How to Build and Manage a
Personal Injury Practice

SECOND EDITION

by K. William Gibson

ABA **LawPracticeManagementSection**
MARKETING • MANAGEMENT • TECHNOLOGY • FINANCE

Commitment to Quality: The Law Practice Management Section is committed to quality in our publications. Our authors are experienced practitioners in their fields. Prior to publication, the contents of all our books are rigorously reviewed by experts to ensure the highest quality product and presentation. Because we are committed to serving our readers' needs, we welcome your feedback on how we can improve future editions of this book.

Cover design by Gail Patejunas.

Nothing contained in this book is to be considered as the rendering of legal advice for specific cases, and readers are responsible for obtaining such advice from their own legal counsel. This book and any forms and agreements herein are intended for educational and informational purposes only.

The products and services mentioned in this publication are under or may be under trademark or service mark protection. Product and service names and terms are used throughout only in an editorial fashion, to the benefit of the product manufacturer or service provider, with no intention of infringement. Use of a product or service name or term in this publication should not be regarded as affecting the validity of any trademark or service mark.

The Law Practice Management Section, American Bar Association, offers an educational program for lawyers in practice. Books and other materials are published in furtherance of that program. Authors and editors of publications may express their own legal interpretations and opinions, which are not necessarily those of either the American Bar Association or the Law Practice Management Section unless adopted pursuant to the bylaws of the Association. The opinions expressed do not reflect in any way a position of the Section or the American Bar Association.

Gibson, K. William, 1949-
  How to build and manage a personal injury practice / by K. William Gibson. – 2nd ed.
      p. cm.
  Includes index.
  ISBN-13: 978-1-59031-673-3
  ISBN-10: 1-59031-673-8
  1. Personal injuries–United States. 2. Practice of law–United States–Management.
I. Title.

  KF1257.G53 2006
  346.7303'23–dc22   2006022985

Library of Congress Cataloging-in-Publication Data is on file.

Discounts are available for books ordered in bulk. Special consideration is given to state bars, CLE programs, and other bar-related organizations. Inquire at Book Publishing, American Bar Association, 321 N. Clark Street, Chicago, Illinois 60610.

Contents

Acknowledgments

I want to first thank my colleagues at the American Bar Association/LPM Publishing for encouraging me to write this second edition. Beverly Loder, in particular, has been a source of sage advice and strong support. She was there to supervise the first edition of this book in 1996. I couldn't have done either edition without her help. Likewise, Tim Johnson and Neal Cox have provided invaluable assistance. These professionals regularly work their magic in producing the best books on law practice management, and I was fortunate to have their help with mine. Their great work makes me look good, and I am grateful.

Thanks, too, go to Reid Trautz and the LPM Publishing Board for their support.

I am especially grateful to my fellow Portland personal injury lawyers, Mike Gutzler and Mike Colbach, for reviewing the manuscript and suggesting changes and additions based on their real-life experiences.

On a personal note, my wife, Mary, gets a big thank you for her encouragement and patience on this and the other two book projects that I have done for the ABA.

Finally, my legal assistant and sister-in-law, Joyce Gibson, did a great job of intercepting phone calls and dealing with clients who wanted my immediate attention while I was writing. Thanks, Joy.

About the Author

K. William Gibson has been a lawyer in Portland, Oregon, since 1980. He was a partner in Gibson & Duffy, a plaintiff's personal injury law firm in Portland, from 1980 until 1988 and has been a solo since then.

He was admitted to the Oregon State Bar in 1979 and has handled only personal injury cases since 1985. He also regularly serves as an arbitrator and mediator in personal injury cases and other disputes.

Mr. Gibson is a longtime member of the ABA Law Practice Management Section and served as chair in 2001–2002. He has served on several ABA committees and commissions and is a member of the ABA Standing Committee on Publishing Oversight.

Mr. Gibson is a regular columnist for *Law Practice* magazine, published by the ABA Law Practice Management Section. He has written numerous articles on law practice management and is a regular speaker at CLE programs. He served as editor of *Flying Solo: A Survival Guide for the Solo and Small Firm Lawyer,* Fourth Edition, also published by the ABA Law Practice Management Section.

He is the founder of De Novo Systems, Inc., a Vancouver, Washington, software company that publishes De Novo CaseMgr, a case management/practice management software system.

Mr. Gibson received a bachelor's degree in political science and a master's degree in industrial and labor relations from the University of Oregon.

Readers can send e-mail to Mr. Gibson at bgibson@cnnw.net.

Introduction

I started practicing law on January 1, 1980. My practice included a law partner, a small office, and a manual typewriter. We did not get our first secretary until a few months later. We bought our first computer in 1984. My partner and I handled criminal defense, collections, domestic relations, bankruptcy, and everything else we could. We represented plaintiffs and we represented defendants.

I had met my law partner a few years earlier when we were law clerks for state court trial judges in Portland, Oregon. Our courtroom experience made us feel comfortable in court, and we both knew that litigation would be a major part of our practice. My partner had been practicing for a few years when we got together, and he brought a few personal injury cases into our new practice.

We saw ourselves as trial lawyers, but we never really had any big victories in those early days. Sometimes we tried the wrong cases and wondered why we lost. Other times we tried good cases but did not do as well as we had expected. Occasionally we obtained good verdicts and felt like we had things figured out. Mostly, though, we tried drunk driving cases. We so wanted to become personal injury lawyers that when someone asked us to take a personal injury case we usually said yes, even if it wasn't such a good case.

For a while, I had three law partners. We all liked litigation work, and if we had focused on building a personal injury practice rather than dabbling in a lot of other areas, we probably would have been very successful and we might still be together. Unfortunately, we couldn't agree on what we wanted to do. We could not even agree to advertise in the Yellow Pages. We only took out a Yellow Pages ad after I threatened to do it on my own if they wouldn't go in on it with me.

Eventually, my law partners went their own ways and I became a solo practitioner. Our longtime secretary quit—probably because she knew that I could not afford her salary. I hired my sister to take her place. My sister did not have any experience, but was looking for an opportunity. I kept the firm's office space and eventually became a landlord for other lawyers. I also got stuck with the bill for the new Yellow Pages ad.

I knew that I really liked personal injury litigation, so I started focusing on building and managing a personal injury practice. I quit taking everything else. I almost starved during my first year as a solo, but I felt like I was moving in the right direction. I explained to my wife that my new strategy for building a personal injury practice was going to mean less income for a while. She was supportive, but nervous. Very nervous.

After my small ad in the Portland Yellow Pages came out, the phone started to ring. I rented a small office from a lawyer friend in a growing suburb about twenty minutes away, keeping my main office in the city. I had no staff in the suburban office, but it was a great place to meet those clients who would not drive downtown just to meet with a lawyer. Next, I took out an ad in that suburb's Yellow Pages so that people would not have to go to the larger metropolitan telephone book.

To my amazement, the phone started to ring in my second office. People called me to help them with their injury claims. Fortunately, the call volume was low enough that I could personally meet with everyone and did not have to add staff. I had seen other plaintiffs' lawyers get killed by their overhead expenses, so I vowed not to overextend myself by adding staff too soon. I still wasn't trying a lot of cases, but I was settling enough of them, either directly with the insurance company or with the aid of a mediator. Arbitration was just becoming popular then, so many of the cases that I could not settle went to arbitration rather than trial. That resulted in cases getting resolved much more quickly and with less cost.

The phone kept on ringing and within two years or so of starting my personal injury practice, I was bringing in enough fees that my wife quit threatening to get a second job. (I think she really thought that I should get a second job, even though she never said so.) I still did everything I could to keep my overhead low. My sister was now my legal assistant and was doing a pretty good job, and I still was not paying her as much as our former secretary had made.

I knew that technology could help me keep my overhead down. I had a computer on my desk and created my own letters and pleadings. We did not have a computer network, so I saved my documents on a floppy disk and gave them to my legal assistant for printing. Our systems were not very sophisticated, but they kept us out of trouble. I had no idea then just how much technology would change over the next few years and how much it would change the way that we practice law. Online legal research, the Internet, e-mail, BlackBerrys, cell phones, and other technology tools that we take for granted today just were not available in the mid-1980s.

Another way that I kept my overhead down was to rent my extra office space to other lawyers. I would not recommend being a landlord to lawyers unless you enjoy negotiating with your tenants about everything under the sun. My tenants were all fine people and good lawyers, but mostly they drove me crazy. Dealing with lawyers can be a little difficult. Thankfully, my stint as a landlord did not last too long.

Seventeen years ago, after I had been on my own for five years, one of my former partners rejoined. He had been working in a political job in city government, and we had remained good friends while he was away. When he came back, we did not make a lot of changes, but we did increase our advertising program and hired another staff person.

We went to a full-page color ad in the Yellow Pages and started running commercials on television. Our call volume increased dramatically, but so did our advertising budget. We liked to say that the Yellow Pages publisher was our "senior partner"; the bill for advertising always got paid before we did, and often was for more than we earned.

In the late '90s my partner and I split up, mostly because I was interested in doing less litigation and more work as an arbitrator and mediator.

After more than twenty-five years of practice, I am often struck by how the personal injury business has changed. With the increased cost of litigation and the increased use of mandatory arbitration, lawyers aren't trying many cases anymore. Increasingly cases are settled through mediation or informal settlement conferences. Most courts now require pretrial settlement conferences with a judge—something that was unheard of even a decade ago. Lawyers who work as in-house counsel for insurance companies generally try more cases than private lawyers, probably because of the volume of cases that they handle, but even those lawyers do not try as many as they used to. One trial judge recently remarked to a group of trial lawyers that "the days of trying the average auto accident case are over."

Young lawyers tell me that they want to become personal-injury lawyers but do not have any cases and do not have enough money to advertise on TV or in the Yellow Pages. I tell them that I faced the same situation when I started, but they have an advantage since they can take advantage of free or low-cost online advertising—a resource that wasn't available when I started.

The fact remains that starting a PI practice takes money and a lot of effort, but building a successful practice takes money and even more effort. It also takes a great deal of patience. It is not going to happen overnight, but it will happen if you want it badly enough.

During my years of practice I periodically ran short of money and wondered if my efforts were going to pay off. Patience was often in short supply. Throughout, however, I knew how much I wanted to make it work and, since I did not want to go to work for anyone else, I knew that I had to make it work.

It is hoped that this book will help *you* make it work.

Why a Personal Injury Practice Is Different

Starting a personal injury practice is not for the faint-hearted. It is different from starting most other types of law practice. The difference is money. (This fact has become even more true since the first edition of this book was published in 1997.) In other types of practice, the lawyer takes in a case, often getting a retainer to cover future fees; does the client's work; sends a bill for the time spent; and then gets paid. In a personal injury practice, the lawyer takes in a case; spends his or her time and money getting the case ready for settlement or trial; and then gets paid in a year or two, if everything goes well. Of course, lawyers who bill hourly also have money problems, such as accounts receivable, but their problems with money don't compare with those faced by Personal Injury (PI) lawyers. PI lawyers, who are on contingency, don't necessarily get paid for all the time that they spend on a case, but if they don't spend enough time, they may not get paid at all.

In a personal injury practice, all cases require a lot of work, and big cases require the most work. Everyone dreams about getting "the big case," only to be shocked to find out how much time and money it requires. Many big cases turn out badly because the plaintiff's lawyer does not spend enough money to hire the doctors, engineers, accident reconstruction experts, and other professionals needed to analyze critical issues and testify in court. Often that is simply because the lawyer does not have the money to invest in the case. Many big cases also turn out badly because the plaintiff's lawyer does not spend enough time to work the case up properly. Often that happens because the lawyer is busy handling other cases, perhaps cases that will generate fees immediately to pay the rent and keep the doors open.

One dilemma behind a personal injury practice is that having a lot of cases can be a problem for you, the PI lawyer, since the more cases you have, the more people you will need to help you work on them. Those people will need to be paid every month, whether you have settled any cases or not. Therefore, you will have to come up with the money to pay them. If it takes two years for the average case to be resolved, you will have to be prepared to meet two years' worth of payroll expenses without settling a case. Are you prepared to do that? How will you come up with that much money? Are you prepared to borrow money? To invest your own money? To sell your house?

If you plan to build a personal injury practice, you will have to face these financial realities. However, do not worry. Once you survive the first couple of years and have generated some cash flow, it becomes much easier. Unfortunately, many aspiring plaintiffs' lawyers have not had enough capital to make it through those first couple of years and are now doing something else for a living. (See Chapter 3 for a discussion of financing your practice.)

Self-Analysis

Given the enormous financial and personal risks involved, you should analyze your personality and your tolerance for risk before undertaking this venture. Not everyone is cut out for it.

That is not to say that PI lawyers all come from the same mold. On the contrary, they come in all personality types. They have different interests and aptitudes, different strengths and weaknesses. Some thrive on courtroom activity, while others prefer to stay out of the courtroom and would rather settle cases. Which do you prefer? Some PI lawyers thrive on high-stakes litigation and are willing to mortgage their homes to finance a good case. Others don't have as high a tolerance for risk. How much would you be willing to risk on a case? High-stakes cases mean long hours at the office, including nights and weekends, for months at a time. Many lawyers are not willing or able to put in that amount of time or to work under that much pressure.

It is, however, quite possible to be a successful personal injury lawyer without handling high-risk, expensive cases. Many lawyers have satisfying careers handling more routine cases and only go to court once or twice a year. Plus, with the increasing popularity of alternative dispute resolution (ADR), including mediation and arbitration, lawyers are trying fewer personal injury cases than in the past. You will be much happier and more successful by starting a practice that suits your own strengths and weaknesses.

In addition, there are alternatives to starting your own practice. If you want to become a malpractice lawyer or handle other high-stakes cases but cannot afford to take the financial risk, you should consider taking a job with a lawyer or firm that handles those cases. The experienced lawyers can teach you how to handle those cases and give you opportunities to work on some cases and perhaps even try cases. Many lawyers have taken that route before going out on their own.

There are other factors to consider as well. Starting a personal injury practice has been made even harder by the insurance and business lobbies' unrelenting assault against injury victims and trial lawyers. Many states, along with the federal government, are implementing "tort reform" legislation that places caps, or upper limits, on the amount that an injured person can recover for punitive damages, as well as for pain and suffering. Some states are limiting the doctrine of joint and several liability in ways that limit an injury victim's right to recover damages from multiple tortfeasors. These reforms have raised the crossbar for plaintiffs, making it harder to obtain a favorable verdict at trial. As a result of their success in the courtroom, insurance companies and corporate defendants are often less motivated to settle before trial, and their pretrial offers are lower than before the reforms took effect.

This means an increase in the percentage of cases in which you will have to file a lawsuit and go through the discovery process. The case that may have been settled quickly in the past will now drag on for months or years until its turn comes for trial. For you that means the added expenses of filing fees, depositions, expert witnesses, and other court costs. For your client it means a long wait before knowing what the outcome will be. Unfortunately, many clients cannot wait the extra time or are simply unwilling to go through a trial, so they end up settling for a fraction of what the case is really worth.

Another phenomenon that does not bode well for the new personal injury practitioner is the public's attitude toward personal injury cases in general. Recent television programs have featured segments on insurance fraud, scams, and conspiracies involving personal injury lawyers, doctors, and their clients. Insurance companies regularly advertise how they are working to reduce fraud to keep premiums low. Large jury awards are trumpeted in headlines across the country. Talk show hosts deride plaintiffs' claims resulting from spilled coffee, errant golf shots, stuck elevators, and the like. Claims for injuries resulting from low-speed auto accidents are routinely being denied by insurance companies and juries are upholding those denials, perhaps suspecting over-treatment or exaggeration. This new public attitude may have weeded out a few dubious claims, but it has emboldened insurance companies and made it harder to get deserving clients the compensation that they are entitled to receive.

So why start a personal injury practice? If it is because you think that it offers the greatest opportunity to get rich, you will be disappointed. You may ultimately get rich, but you would be more likely to achieve the same or greater wealth by investing your time and money in real estate or any number of other ventures not connected to the practice of law. Even though the ranks of plaintiffs' lawyers include a number of high-profile, high-income lawyers, thousands more lawyers across the county toil in obscurity and make unremarkable incomes.

On the bright side, however, is the fact that nowhere in the practice of law is there a greater opportunity to help those who are truly in need—who have been wronged through no fault of their own and who are not going to get any relief without a lawyer who is willing to fight for their rights. Nowhere in the practice of law is there more of a David versus Goliath scenario than a working man or woman or retired person or child doing battle with a gigantic insurance company or corporation.

Any lawyer who has taken a deserving client's case through the legal system all the way to trial and has ridden out the waves of delay, obfuscation, and occasional deception knows that there is no better feeling in the world than having put up with all that abuse from the other side and finally having his or her cause validated by a jury. When that happens to you, your client is convinced that you are the best lawyer on the planet; the opposing lawyers have to concede that you might possibly know what you are doing; and you gain a measure of confidence and self-assurance that will keep you in the game for a while longer. You will only be able to enjoy those moments occasionally, and then only if you have managed your practice wisely.

Lawyers who fail to build a successful personal injury practice often point to poor case selection, mismanagement of personnel, and poor use of time and money. No lawyer starts a practice intending to fail, but many start a practice doomed to failure because the practice has not been built on a sound foundation. There are four cornerstones of that sound foundation:

1. A commitment to work hard to make your practice succeed
2. The ability to manage your time, money, and people
3. Adequate capital
4. The desire to do the right thing for your clients

If these cornerstones are in place, success will follow. This maxim is equally true whether you are new to the private practice of law, are an experienced PI lawyer, or are thinking of adding personal injury cases to your established practice.

Your First Big Decision: Solo Practice or Partnership?

2

ONE OF THE MOST IMPORTANT DECISIONS that you will make in preparing to open your personal injury practice is whether to go it alone—to practice as a solo—or to form a partnership with another lawyer, or perhaps with several other lawyers.

These choices assume that you have decided that the time is right to start your own practice. You first need to decide if this is, in fact, the right time to go out on your own. It may be that the time is not right. Maybe you do not have the resources to finance the practice. Maybe you cannot afford to wait until your cases start to pay off. Maybe you have other commitments that will prevent you from spending the time that a new practice would require. If the time is not right to start your own practice, this would be the perfect time to acknowledge that fact, rather than reaching that conclusion after spending a great deal of time and money to open the doors. Just because the time is not right to go out on your own doesn't mean that you can't become a personal injury lawyer. In fact, you may be one already, but if you are not an experienced personal injury lawyer, this may be a perfect time to learn your craft by working for more experienced lawyers.

There are several options if you decide to go that route. The first option is to go to work for another plaintiff's law firm (or for a solo who needs help.) Many of the best PI lawyers whom I have met have honed their skills by working with a more experienced lawyer; then they either have taken over that lawyer's practice or have gone out alone after a few years. A second option is to go to work for a firm that does insurance defense work. Several of the finest plaintiffs' lawyers I know are former defense lawyers. A job with a defense firm would give you a paid opportunity to learn the PI business inside and out. You would quickly learn how the defense business works and, at the same time, you would have a unique vantage point from which to watch the plaintiff's bar at work. You would quickly learn what it takes to win cases at trial or settle cases for top value. A third option would be to go to work for a corporation or governmental agency doing litigation. Since they are usually self-insured, many government lawyers keep busy defending injury claims. It is the same with corporations—many businesses have in-house counsel to defend lawsuits that are, for whatever reason, not covered by insurance and handled by the insurance company's lawyers.

If you do decide that the time is right to strike out on your own, think carefully about taking on a partner at the beginning.

To Partner or Not?

You have probably heard the expression that a partnership is "like a marriage." Like many old sayings, this one has a lot of truth to it. Whether to have a partner and, just as importantly, who that partner will be are decisions that will affect your life and practice for years to come.

Just as it is important to assess your personality in deciding whether to become a PI lawyer in the first place, deciding whether to practice on your own as a solo or to form a partnership with another lawyer takes even more self-analysis. Since it is more common for someone starting a personal injury practice to form a partnership with one other person rather than with more than one person, this discussion will focus on a partnership of only two lawyers. Everything discussed here applies to a partnership of three or more as well, except that the problems become exponentially more complicated as more partners are involved.

Advantages of a Solo Practice

Many entrepreneurs are better suited to solo practice than to working in an organization, whether that be a law firm, a corporation, or a government agency. That is simply because they have a need to make all the decisions and have things their way all the time. When other people have an interest in any issue, whether they are partners, co-workers or bosses, they must be consulted and their opinions considered before decisions are made. In many cases they even get to have the final say in what gets decided.

When you have an equal partner in your law practice, that person is entitled, legally and otherwise, to an equal say in all decisions made by the partnership. If you are considering joining with a partner, the first question you must ask is whether you are willing to give someone that great a voice in your practice. If your answer is no, don't even think about a partner. You are probably better off practicing on your own.

Life as a solo is less structured than life in an organization. Solos don't need to have as many meetings. Solos don't need to get someone else's okay before buying a computer. Solos don't have to be concerned about what someone else (the partner) thinks about everything. Solos don't have to share. In most partnerships, the partners share in the revenues and expenses. Solos, on the other hand, get to keep everything they bring in. If you are someone who has difficulty sharing your bounty with others, you are probably not well suited for a partnership.

A solo practice doesn't need as much to get by as a partnership does. Solos often work out of a small office, sometimes an executive suite arrangement, with a minimal amount of staff. For some reason, partnerships tend to have more office space, more staff, and more fixed overhead. Perhaps it is because partnerships think of themselves as "law firms" and feel it is necessary to have all the appropriate trappings. Perhaps it is because partnerships can take advantage of economies of scale on everything from staff to supplies and can afford resources that are too expensive for a solo. The many factors involved in a solo practice are discussed in *Flying Solo: A Survival Guide for the Solo Lawyer,* Fourth Edition, (American Bar Association, Law Practice Management Section, 2005).

Disadvantages of a Solo Practice

The biggest disadvantage of being a solo is that you work alone and are often isolated. When things are going badly, there is nobody to talk to about it. When revenues are down and someone has to put money into the practice, that someone is you and you alone. When that big case that you put a lot of time and money into goes bust, you are the one who takes the loss. If you had a partner bringing in money while you were gambling on your long shot, the financial effect of losing would not be nearly as serious.

Advantages of a Partnership

The advantages of a partnership are both financial and social. The main financial advantages of a partnership are that there are two people to bring in resources and generate fees and to share the expenses. This means that neither partner has sole responsibility for either bringing in revenue or paying the office expenses, and if one partner has a bad month, the other one may be able to make up the difference. Considering the financial risk associated with a contingent fee-based practice, having someone to take on half the risk should give you some peace of mind. Since both partners are sharing the risk, they have an obligation to talk with each other before taking on an expensive or risky case. The process of talking over such decisions can help avoid taking on too much risk. Without someone to challenge, or at least question, his or her decisions, the solo is more likely to make decisions on the "spur of the moment," only to regret it later. Solos who share office space can often get feedback and advice from other lawyers, but the advice of someone who has a direct stake in the decision is probably more sound than that of someone who has no interest in the situation.

The main social advantage of a partnership is that there is someone else with whom you can share both the good times and bad times in your practice. If you enjoy and need that kind of sharing, you are probably better suited for a partnership than a solo practice.

Having a partner will also allow you to take vacations, knowing that your partner will be in the office to handle emergencies. For a solo, a legal secretary or legal assistant can usually take care of most things that come up during your absence and can arrange for another lawyer to cover an unexpected court appearance. Having a partner, however, means that you can arrange for your partner to cover a deposition or other proceeding while you are away on your vacation. You, of course, will provide the same cover for your partner when he or she is away. Having a partner means that you won't have to clear your calendar completely to get away for a week or two. If you plan to take vacations and want to have the peace of mind of knowing that someone will be looking out for your cases, a partnership might be just what you need.

Partnerships are also better during times of illness or crisis. It is one thing for a solo to ask another lawyer to cover a brief court appearance, but it is another thing altogether to ask someone to cover your entire practice while you are recovering from an illness or a death in the family. For that kind of assistance you need a partner. (In addition, you need disability insurance to cover your lost income and your share of the office expenses while you are away.) It is not that a partner will give your cases the same amount of attention that you would, but at least something will be done to make sure that the case is not lost or that the client does not fire you while you are away.

The death of a solo practitioner creates some particularly difficult problems for the survivors. Many jurisdictions prohibit the sale of a practice by a solo, so upon the lawyer's death the family is faced with the problem of arranging for new counsel for the clients, without having any prospects of being compensated when those cases are finally resolved. In a partnership, the estate of the deceased partner can be compensated for cases that the partnership was working on, but had not yet settled, at the time of the partner's death.

Taking on a Partner

Personal injury lawyers practice as solos and in large firms and everything in between. One advantage of practicing alone is that you get to make all the decisions and do not have to be accountable to other "co-owners." However, a corresponding disadvantage is that there is no one else to help you pay the cost of implementing all your decisions. Two or more partners working together can share the costs of starting up and managing a practice more easily than one lawyer can working alone. It is one of the main reasons that lawyers form partnerships.

There are two primary reasons why having a partner will help you get financing for your practice:

1. Your partner may have additional resources to use as collateral to secure a loan.
2. A lender will feel more secure about having two people on the hook for the loan rather than having just one person.

If you decide to team up with one or more other lawyers to start a personal injury practice, you will first have to decide how to structure the relationship. At this point, you will probably need some outside advice. The important issues include the legal structure of your relationship and the written agreement that describes the terms of the relationship. Take the time to reduce your agreement to writing and have all parties sign it. You will be looking at three options:

1. **Partnership:** This is the most common form for doing business with someone else. It is relatively simple to have agreements drafted, and there are standard partnership agree-

ments readily available from the American Bar Association (ABA) and your state or local bar association. A partnership does not have to be a fifty-fifty arrangement. The arrangement can be whatever you decide, provided that it is within the bounds of state and federal partnership laws. Be aware that one of the major disadvantages of the partnership form is that each partner may be held liable for the debts of the other partner and the consequences that arise from that partner's professional negligence or wrongdoing.

2. **Professional Corporation (P.C.):** Many states now permit professional service organizations to be formed as a professional corporation. While many of the original tax benefits available to shareholders of a P.C. have disappeared, it is still possible to purchase health insurance with pretax dollars and to contribute pretax into retirement plans. P.C.s also limit the personal liability of each shareholder.

3. **Limited Liability Partnerships (LLP) or Corporations (LLC):** LLPs and LLCs are statutory creations, and their applicability to law practices varies from state to state. The main advantage of limited liability organizations is the limitations on personal liability that they provide to individual members of the organization.

Choosing the Right Partner

The person you form a partnership with must be someone who, above all, can be trusted. Just as with the person you choose to marry, a prospective partner should be someone you know and trust. Anyone can make a good impression over a short period of time, but few people can hide their true character for a long time. When considering prospects for partnership, talk with their former partners or others who know them better than you do. If their most recent partnership ended acrimoniously, then a conversation with former partners will be no more objective than a conversation with a former spouse. Nonetheless, it is important to check their references.

There are many other qualities that you should look for in a prospective partner in a personal injury practice. On a personal level he or she should be truthful, ethical, considerate of other people, compassionate, slow to anger, and unselfish. He or she should be someone you like and respect and whose company you enjoy. On a professional level, look for qualities such as a good work ethic, diligence, thoroughness, a willingness to fight for clients, and the ability to present a case effectively. Your prospective partner should also be a good "team player." Just as you need to recognize whether your personality is better suited to solo practice, you need to recognize whether a prospective partner is really suited to be in a partnership. Sometimes the good solo makes a bad partner.

It is not necessary that a prospective partner and you have the same type of personality, but it is important that your personalities and personal styles don't conflict with each other. There are several factors to consider in this light.

Compatibility

Select a partner who has the same goals for the practice as you have. If your goals and objectives are not similar, you will face a lot of conflict and may never reach agreement on where the practice should go. If you want to have a small, easygoing kind of practice, you should avoid someone who wants to build an empire. If you want to expand into neighboring communities and advertise on television, you will not want a partner who prefers a low-profile practice. Your partner should have the same financial objectives as you. Assuming that the personal injury practice will be your primary source of income, avoid someone who could just as easily live on his or her trust fund or investment income. You should both have the same level of financial need and desire for income. Of course, if you both have trust funds or are otherwise independently wealthy, you may be perfectly compatible.

Work Habits

Some people like to work more than other people. Many lawyers are workaholics—they would rather work than do just about anything else. Other lawyers prefer to work less and to participate in outside activities. Your prospective partner should have the same general work habits as you. If one partner works night and day and the other does not, there is a potential for friction, especially if the workaholic partner expects everyone to share his or her work habits. On the other hand, it is possible that two partners with different work styles can actually complement each other and balance each other in the office.

Power Sharing

Some people find it necessary to be in control in their relationships, and lawyers are certainly no exception. Many partnerships have failed because the partners could not find a satisfactory way to share power in the partnership. Look for a partner who is willing and able to share power with you. If you are constantly battling each other for power and control, your attention will be diverted from your cases and your relationship with your partner will not last. If you know that you are someone who must be in control, you may be fortunate enough to find a partner who is willing to let you make all the decisions. Some people don't want to be burdened with the responsibility of running a law practice and are quite happy to give that responsibility to a partner.

Good Communication

The keys to a successful law partnership are mutual goals, compatible styles, and good communication. If you are considering starting a practice with someone, first spend a lot of time discussing your goals and styles. Be truthful about your expectations. If there are any areas of contention, this is the time to get them out in the open—not after you have started a practice together. Before you form the partnership, reach an agreement about the importance of good communication and agree to meet regularly, both together and with your staff, to discuss issues of mutual importance.

If your prospective partner is not a good communicator, or does not value communication, you should reconsider going into practice with that person. Most trial lawyers are good at communicating with judges and juries, so there is no reason why they can't communicate just as well with a prospective law partner. Most communication problems are not caused by an inability to communicate but rather by a lack of willingness to do so. The trial lawyer who is not willing to exercise good communication in a law practice should probably be practicing alone.

Issues to Discuss

There are a number of issues that need to be resolved before a partnership is formed, including the following:

1. What will be the name of the partnership? Smith & Jones or Jones & Smith?
2. Where will your office be located? How many offices will you have? If you have multiple offices, who will work where?
3. Will you have a fancy office or a plain one? What if one partner wants expensive furniture and the other partner wants budget furniture? Should the difference in cost be borne by the lawyer or by the partnership?
4. Do both of you have the same philosophy about advertising and marketing? How much are you going to invest in advertising?
5. How much of a financial commitment are you each willing and able to make to the partnership? Are you willing to invest your own money or to borrow money?
6. How much of a salary or draw do you need to live on during the startup phase of the practice? What are your long-term financial expectations from the practice? How do you prefer to divide up the profits? Do you want to share the profits equally or should they be divided according to how much each partner brings in? Should it be a fifty-fifty partnership or something else?
7. Do both of you want to build the same kind of practice? Does one of you want a high-volume practice and the other want a big-case, specialty practice? If so, are these objectives compatible? Do you want to handle specialized cases involving medical malpractice and products liability? What about related cases such as employment law and securities fraud?

8. What is your philosophy about advancing costs for clients who cannot afford to pay for ongoing case expenses? Do you agree that the partnership will advance costs in all cases? In some cases? If so, which cases?

9. What is your philosophy about trying cases versus settling before trial? Do both of you like to try cases? Does one of you like to try cases more than the other? Is one of you better at trying cases than the other?

10. What is your philosophy about alternative dispute resolution (ADR) methods such as mediation and arbitration?

11. How does each of you view your time commitment to the practice? Are you each willing to work as much as necessary to make the practice a success? What if one of you is a workaholic and the other likes to take time off? If one of you likes to work weekends, do you expect the other to be in the office too? Do both of you like to take vacations? If so, how many weeks a year?

12. Do you have the same philosophy about technology? Is one of you more computer literate than the other? Does the non-computer-literate partner recognize the need for technology in the office? Is that partner willing to spend what it takes to have a state-of-the-art office? Is that partner willing to learn to use technology?

13. Do you have compatible styles of working with staff? Does one partner need a disproportionate amount of staff? Is the need for more staff tied to an unwillingness to use technology? Are you both willing to make your support staff part of the team? Do you both work well with staff? Do either of you go through a lot of staff?

14. Do you both have the same attitude about professionalism? Do you have the same view of the role of the lawyer in litigation?

15. What happens if one of you decides to leave the partnership? How will you provide for that partner's withdrawal? What happens if one of you is injured or becomes ill and cannot work for a long period of time? What happens if one of you dies?

The many issues involved in setting up a partnership are discussed in detail in *Flying Solo: A Survival Guide for the Solo and Small Firm Lawyer*, Fourth Edition (American Bar Association, Law Practice Management Section, 2005).

Resolving Disputes

Problems arise in a partnership just as they do in a marriage or any other relationship between people. When those problems are not resolved, there are both personal and financial consequences. When a partnership dissolves unexpectedly, the partners are forced to spend time dealing with the breakup when that time could be better spent settling cases or getting ready for trial.

You should have a written partnership agreement and it should provide for mediation in case you encounter problems that you cannot work out on your own. Many state bar associations have programs to provide counseling and mediation for a wide variety of problems faced by lawyers. (One bar association mediator even reported mediating a dispute between a solo and his secretary over pay and working conditions.) A trained mediator can often help the disputing parties identify the issues that are causing disagreement and explore solutions with which everyone can live. Mediation can often make the difference between dissolution and survival of the partnership.

Planning for Your New Practice | **3**

BEFORE OPENING THE OFFICE DOORS, you must have a good business plan. While it is true that a new personal injury lawyer could scare up enough money to pay the first month's expenses and then just work hard and hope for the best, that approach is not really advisable. Having a business plan will take the guesswork out of the process of opening an office. More importantly, though, a business plan will force that new lawyer to confront the realities associated with starting *any* small business or professional office.

According to Linda Pinson, author of a software package entitled *The Lawyer's Guide to Creating a Business Plan: A Step-by-Step Software Package* (American Bar Association, 2005), there are two main benefits that will flow from the preparation of a carefully written business plan. Those benefits are

1. To serve as a guide for your business. Pinson says that "the business plan is a blueprint of your business and will provide you with the

tools to analyze your business and implement changes that will make your business more profitable."

2. As documentation for financing. Pinson observes that "a business plan is a requirement if you are planning to seek financing. If you are seeking capital, the business plan details how the desired investment or loan will further the company's goals and increase its profits."

In my view, your business plan should include six key elements:

1. A description of the kinds of services you intend to offer
2. A statement of the location(s) where you plan to offer your services
3. A description of your target market (i.e., who will use your services)
4. A projection of anticipated revenue and operating expenses
5. A statement of personal resources that you intend to commit to financing the practice
6. Statements detailing your personal net worth—that is, assets (bank account balances; stock holdings; value of home, car, and other personal property; etc.) and liabilities (amounts owed on credit cards, student loans, etc.)

Linda Pinson's software package, which includes a PDF version of her book, *Anatomy of a Business Plan,* automates the process of creating a business plan and allows even a novice personal injury lawyer to create a professional-looking and well thought-out plan. Using a program such as Pinson's takes the guesswork out of the process and provides you with a professional-quality plan that will be sure to impress readers.

Getting Financial Advice

A major portion of your business plan will be projections about revenue, expenses, and the additional costs required to finance your cases. It is probably a good idea to hire an outsider to help you prepare your business plan. Before preparing your business plan, even if you use a software tool such as the one Linda Pinson offers with her book, you will still need to make a number of operational and financial assumptions. Before meeting with a bank or other potential lender, I would suggest that you seek guidance on preparing your business plan. Some sources of guidance include the following:

- ◆ **Established PI lawyers:** Go to your local or state bar association or trial lawyers' organization to seek assistance from other personal injury lawyers who may be willing to lend you a hand by sharing their experiences in starting a practice. Many bar organizations have mentoring programs designed for just that purpose. The assistance of an experienced lawyer will be invaluable in forecasting the potential out-of-pocket costs involved in personal injury cases. An experienced lawyer may also be willing to share with you the names of vendors and experts with whom you can work.

- ◆ **Your Certified Public Accountant (CPA):** The involvement of an accountant gives your business plan immediate credibility with potential lenders. Your CPA will make sure that your plan makes financial sense and is in proper form. In addition, your CPA will be able to tell you exactly what you need to do to comply with the rules and regulations of the Internal Revenue Service (IRS) and other government agencies.

- ◆ **Bar association practice management advisors:** Many state and local bar associations have practice advisors—professionals who provide free advice and assistance to lawyers in private practice. Many practice advisors are former practicing lawyers or law office administrators who have been through what you are now going through and thus can offer a wealth of information and advice. They can also help you access other information and resources that might be available through bar associations or government agencies.

- ◆ **Small Business Administration (SBA) (*www.sba.gov*):** The federal government and many states provide free or low-cost assistance and counseling to small businesses through the Small Business Administration, state economic development offices and local business assistance centers. Other resources include local colleges and universities. Law school placement offices can be another source of information.

Developing a Financial Forecast: Expense Projections

Before opening the doors to your new practice, you will need to know how much it is going to cost to run the practice. Anyone thinking about lending you money to open the doors will want to know the same thing. The first question that a PI lawyer starting out must answer is how much cash will be required to start the law practice. The second question is how much additional cash will be required to finance cases. And, the third question is how much salary the lawyer will need to meet normal living expenses during the startup phase of building the practice. After you answer these questions, you will be in a better position to forecast how much money you will need and when you will need it. You will be able to provide your forecasts to prospective lenders or financial advisors.

Startup Expenses

You will need to pay for the things you need to start your practice as well as for ongoing expenses once you open the doors. The following are some of the items to consider:

- ◆ Office space (which may require a down payment or deposit)
- ◆ Furniture and office decorations
- ◆ Telephone equipment
- ◆ Telephone lines and directory listings
- ◆ Yellow Pages and Internet advertising
- ◆ Web site development costs
- ◆ Malpractice insurance
- ◆ Equipment, including a computer, printer, photocopier, and fax machine
- ◆ Law books and periodicals

- ◆ Internet expenses
- ◆ Stationery, business cards, announcements, and postage
- ◆ Other office supplies
- ◆ Secretarial services

Potential lenders will want to know that you have considered each of these items in your budget. Be sure to identify those items that you intend to purchase outright and those that you plan to lease.

Ongoing Expenses

Your largest ongoing expense categories will be office rent, employee salaries, and advertising and marketing. You won't succeed unless you get these expenses under control and, more importantly, keep them under control as time goes on. Seventy percent of the cost of operating a law firm goes toward rent, payroll, advertising and marketing, client costs, malpractice insurance, and interest on debt. Here are some ways in which you can control and forecast expenses in some of those major categories.

Rent Expenses

The first expense category that you will need to budget for is office rent. The problem with rent is that it comes due every month. Chapter 4 contains several options to cut down on rent expenses, such as a home office, executive suite, or sublease.

Whichever way you decide to proceed, be sure that you have enough money available to pay the rent during the lean months.

Employee Salaries

Another expense category that you will have to forecast is employee salaries. Your local bar association or private legal placement companies will be able to provide you with information on salaries and benefits to allow you to make an estimate of what it will cost.

An alternative to hiring a full-time secretary or legal assistant is to hire someone part-time and pay him or her on an hourly basis. You will find that there are secretaries and legal assistants who prefer to work part-time or on a flexible schedule with varying hours because they have other interests or responsibilities. If you are using an executive suite for your office and don't have space for a secretary, you may be able to find a secretary who can work out of his or her home and save you the cost of providing office space.

Advertising and Marketing

Advertising and marketing is one expense category over which you have total control. You can budget it at zero—although at that level you won't see much benefit from your advertising and marketing program—or you can spend enough to get a full-page ad in your metropolitan Yellow Pages directory. With a full-page ad in the Yellow Pages costing a small fortune and requiring a full-year commitment, this is the item that will put you out of business if you are not careful. The best advice concerning Yellow Pages is that while you should definitely have a presence there, you should not have more of a presence than you can afford. To put it another way, a small ad is better than no ad, but an ad that you can't pay for is the same as no ad at all.

Client Costs

Many lawyers who are starting their own personal injury practice don't have a lot of cases requiring large monetary expenditures. In fact, they may not have any cases at all. As soon as they get a few cases, though, they will need to spend their own money to finance those cases.

The average case—usually a small to medium-sized case—will only require a large expenditure of money if it has to be taken to trial. Trials are expensive.

Unless your case requires expert analysis by a doctor, engineer, or other professional, your expenditures may be limited to the costs of police reports, limited accident investigation, medical reports, filing fees, and depositions.

One of the most expensive items in any case is the cost of your client's doctor's testimony. Small cases cannot usually justify the expense of having a doctor testify "live" in court. Fortunately, doctor's records and reports can often substitute for live testimony. Videotaped depositions, while not as desirable as live testimony, are often a less expensive compromise between producing live testimony and simply introducing reports and records.

Personal Expenses

If you have parents, a spouse, or a significant other who will support you while you are getting your practice off the ground, you are fortunate. If you plan on supporting yourself while building your PI practice, you need to know how much you will need each month and include that amount in your business plan.

Make a list of all your personal expenses, just as you made a list of your projected office expenses. Include your rent or mortgage, health insurance, car payment, and other expenses, including the occasional night out. While you are making your list, consider whether there are any expenses that can be reduced for a couple of years while you get your practice going. Ask yourself whether you can really afford the car that you bought when you graduated from law school; whether your membership in the health club is truly necessary; whether you should defer any expensive vacations that you have planned; and whether you can reduce your rent or mortgage payment until things get rolling.

Lenders

Your next step will be to find a source of funding. Lenders, especially bankers, are quite conservative and will likely want to see the level of investment that you are willing to put into your practice as well as the level of sacrifice that you are willing to make. Most lenders will not want to be the sole source of financing for your new firm, and they won't want to be the sole source of your salary. Be prepared for rejection and be prepared to shop around for the best deal. Most importantly, be prepared with the facts and figures to show that you know what this venture will cost and that you are willing to make whatever commitment it takes to make it work.

You may be asked to put up some collateral and, depending on your present circumstances, you may be asked for information

about your earnings history, personal net worth, prior relationships with the bank, and other factors. Be prepared to give a security interest in your home, your car, your retirement account, and
any other substantial assets you might have. To the extent that you
can show that you are investing a greater amount than the lender,
you will more likely be able to negotiate a lower collateral or a
lower interest rate.

Developing a Financial Forecast: Revenue Projections

Forecasting revenue is always the most difficult part of developing
any business plan. Lenders will not be impressed by an overly opti-
mistic estimate of projected revenue. You will be better off pro-
jecting your income at a low level during the first year of operation
and then gradually increasing it during the second and third year
as your caseload increases and the pipeline fills up.

The lender will expect your business plan to show an increase
in projected revenues over time. Your task will be to show that
increase in a realistic and thoughtful manner. If you can show how
you plan to keep your costs under control, you will only need to
project enough income to pay back your loan and to pay yourself
a modest salary. On the other hand, if your business plan shows a
dramatic increase in expenses over time, your revenue forecasts
had better keep pace or you might not get your financing. Therefore, you may need to consider some ways to improve your revenue projections.

Non-Personal Injury Cases

You may be able to improve your revenue projections by showing
revenue from cases other than personal injury cases. A lender
might be impressed that you are so willing to make your practice
succeed that you are willing to handle other cases until the PI
cases start to bear fruit. Most personal injury lawyers began by
handling non-PI cases or by working in a firm that paid them to
handle PI cases only. If you need to handle cases other than PI

cases, by all means do so. Divorce or criminal or bankruptcy cases can help pay the bills.

There are more drastic alternatives. Some aspiring personal injury lawyers have even worked as waiters or teachers or have sold cars while they were building their practices.

Planning for Growth

As your personal injury practice grows, you may eventually want to add more staff, open another office, begin handling different kinds of cases, or expand your marketing and advertising. Each of these activities can help your practice grow and prosper, but if the activities are not wisely planned and budgeted, they can actually set your practice back by overextending your finances. As part of your business plan, these long-term issues should be identified and explored. For example, if you decide to add more staff, what will it cost per person? The same question should be addressed regarding adding office space. By planning for such expenses and knowing what the costs will be, you won't be surprised by unanticipated expenses at some point in the future, and you won't be tempted to act impulsively.

Planning for Market Trends

Your financial planning should address any anticipated changes in the market as a result of legislation or other factors. Many state legislatures have implemented some form of tort reform or legal reform that impairs the ability of individuals in those states to bring actions for personal injuries. Such legislative changes, if implemented in your jurisdiction, could wreak havoc on your financial planning and should be anticipated.

Feast or Famine

Any financial plan for a personal injury practice should recognize that the annual income of a full-time PI lawyer goes through wild swings over the course of a career. It is difficult to smooth out the cash flow curve when you have so little control over when a case will settle or be tried. The tendency of most PI lawyers is to take out too much of the available cash during the good times without planning for the next down cycle. Any financial advisor will tell you to take a conservative approach to taking draws out of available profits. As a solo practitioner or a partner, you will have to pay income taxes on the undistributed cash even if you don't take it as a draw. That fact makes it easy to rationalize taking out more money than you would if it weren't going to be taxed.

Some expenses can be prepaid for the coming year and taken as expenses in the current year. By prepaying those expenses, you reduce your taxable income in the current year and also reduce your expenses for the next year.

Planning for Retirement

Solo and small firm lawyers can also reduce their taxable incomes by putting a portion of their available profits into retirement plans. How much money you can set aside for retirement will depend on whether you are a solo practitioner, a shareholder in a professional corporation, or a partner in a partnership. If you are young and starting your own practice, you can shorten the time to retirement by regularly making tax-deductible contributions into a qualified retirement plan from the beginning of your career. If you have been practicing a while, you already know that you need to provide for your retirement and that it is never too late to begin making regular contributions.

Financial planners, accountants, and tax lawyers, as well as stockbrokers and life insurance agents, can offer you a wealth of information.

Going All the Way

In the beginning, your objective will be to get your office opened and to begin attracting and serving clients. Your next objective will be to serve your clients so well that you begin getting paid and no longer need to subsidize your practice. Your long-term objective will be to have an excess of revenue over expenses so that you can pay yourself and not just everyone else. Moving through these stages will test your will. Just when you feel that you have comfortably reached the third stage and have been getting a regular paycheck for a few months, the well may unexpectedly go dry. Cases that you were positive would settle for a lot of money suddenly go bad. Cases that were certain to be tried in April get reset for December. All of a sudden, there is no money for that paycheck to which you've gotten so accustomed. That is when both your will and your sense of humor will be tested. If you make it that far, success will not be far behind.

Office Space and $\Big|$ **4**
Equipment

Y OU WILL NEED OFFICE SPACE with appropriate furnishings and technology in order to operate a productive and successful personal injury practice. There are several options when it comes to choosing office space and numerous considerations when it comes to purchasing equipment.

Choosing Office Space

Every lawyer needs an office (even if it is at home), but every office is different. The office you will need will depend, in part, on the type of practice the lawyer has.

How are the office needs of a personal injury lawyer different from those of other lawyers? To begin with, unlike some business lawyers and litigators, you don't need to impress corporate clients with a lot of marble and mahogany in an expensive high-rise. Your clients are going to form their opinion of you based on how well you seem to know what you are doing, not on your decor. And you won't need your office to impress the lawyers on the other side. You will only see them in a conference room at a deposition or arbitration or in a courtroom at a trial. They are going to form their opinion of you based on the kind of job you do in representing your clients.

That is not to say that appearance isn't important. Your office needs to be presentable, and it needs to project a professional image to visitors, but beyond that it needs to be a comfortable place in which to work. It should be functional and large enough so that your staff can get their work done. Your office should also be accessible to your clients, some of whom will have disabilities that prevent them from climbing stairs. Offices in older, converted houses often do not have elevators, and even getting from the street into the first-floor reception area can be difficult, if not impossible.

Leasing Your Own Office Suite

Leasing an office suite is the option that most lawyers and law firms select. It probably is not going to be the most cost-effective option for you if you are starting a practice by yourself or with only one secretary or assistant. Most office leases are entered into directly with the owner of the office building, sometimes through a leasing agent, but occasionally lawyers can sublease space from an existing tenant or lessee. Building owners usually require multi-year leases with three- to five-year terms being quite common. If you are considering subleasing from an existing lessee, be sure to check the terms of the lease to find out whether subleases are allowed and whether the owner (or lessor) has to give approval to the sublease. One advantage of subleasing is that you may be able to negotiate a rent that is below the market rate.

Subleasing from Lawyers

Lawyers often have excess office space because a partner leaves or retires or because they leased more space than they really needed. In those cases, they will often sublease an office to other lawyers, either on a month-to-month tenancy or for the remaining time on their lease. Such arrangements usually include reception services for their clients but not telephone answering or secretarial services, although there are exceptions.

Sharing Office Space

It is common for a group of lawyers to lease office space. Office sharing is different from subleasing because all lawyers are usually obligated on the lease. Such an arrangement can also involve sharing employees, with the same options as previously discussed. One of the benefits of sharing space is that all the lawyers share expenses. PI lawyers can develop referrals by sharing space with lawyers who do not handle PI cases. One consideration in sharing office space is to make sure that you are not legally liable for obligations of the lawyer from whom you are renting. This includes payroll and personnel matters, such as unemployment and workers' compensation claims and harassment or discrimination claims. It also includes malpractice claims against the other lawyer. Make it clear to the public that you are not a law firm or partnership, but are separate legal entities.

According to law office consultant Nancy Byerly Jones (writing in *Flying Solo: A Survival Guide for the Solo and Small Firm Lawyer,* Fourth Edition), if you are considering sharing an office, the "must do" list includes the following:

1. Have a written office-sharing agreement.
2. Inform and educate clients.
3. Avoid partnership-like actions or appearances.
4. Protect client confidentiality at all times.
5. Be respectful of others' property and space.

Byerly Jones gives a checklist of agreement terms, including

◆ a requirement that all lawyers carry professional liability insurance (required in most states);
◆ an agreement to try to avoid taking adversarial positions against others in the office;
◆ a clear understanding regarding the use and maintenance of shared office equipment;
◆ a similar understanding regarding sharing office personnel and the development of personnel policies;
◆ a detailed outline of all financial responsibilities; and
◆ terms for handling a dissolution of the office sharing arrangement.

Using a Home Office

More and more lawyers have a home office. Most also have an office elsewhere, but many lawyers have their only office at home. For those lawyers, there are two problems that must be dealt with: (1) how to separate work from home and family life when both are taking place in the same space and time, and (2) where to meet clients.

Creating space and time to work at home requires physical and mental separation from family affairs for periods of time during the day. The problem is the same for all lawyers trying to work at home. The home office should be something more than the dining room table, and it should have a door that can be closed so that telephone conversations can proceed in private and undisturbed by the family dog's barking. Meetings with clients can be arranged at other locations, such as executive suites, borrowed offices, or even coffee shops.

Most lawyers practicing from home do so out of economic necessity, and most also give the home office mixed reviews. The advantages are that the lawyer doesn't have to commute and can "go to work" in pajamas if necessary. The disadvantages include the fact that the lawyer is isolated from colleagues. Many lawyers who begin with only a home office eventually rent another space, such as an executive suite, even if only on a part-time basis.

The economic savings associated with working from home can be quite dramatic. In addition to saving on rent, such expensive items as parking, fuel expenses, and wear and tear on your car can be drastically reduced.

A legal problem may arise for lawyers who have a home office in one state and another office in a second state, but only if their secretary or assistant performs any work in the state where the lawyer's home is located. You, the lawyer, may be required to report a portion of your staff's salaries to your home state and be responsible for meeting workers' compensation insurance requirements of *both states.*

In determining whether a home office is right for you, I would recommend that you consider the following factors discussed in detail by author Diane L. Drain in *Flying Solo: A Survival Guide for the Solo and Small Firm Lawyer,* Fourth Edition:

- ◆ Your personal needs
- ◆ Your professional needs
- ◆ Your emotional needs
- ◆ The geographic location of your home
- ◆ The physical layout of your home
- ◆ The balance of life and work
- ◆ Security and privacy
- ◆ Expectation of clients
- ◆ Zoning

Purchasing Office Space

If you find an area where you want to locate and stay for a long time, consider purchasing office space. The most common way that lawyers buy an office is to buy an existing small office or converted house, but many lawyers have purchased "office condominiums." In the office condominium, each lawyer owns an individual office and pays a monthly maintenance fee to cover expenses and to pay for common areas.

For many lawyers planning for retirement, the sale of an office building that they purchased thirty or forty years ago will probably pay for their retirement. Many lawyers have done well buying and then later selling their office building, but other lawyers have lost money. It all depends on the market, but historically, real estate values, particularly commercial buildings, have appreciated over time throughout the country. Whether buying an office is a viable alternative for you will depend on a number of factors, including location, interest rates, and market timing.

A real estate professional or a CPA can advise you regarding the financial and tax advantages of buying versus leasing office space. The main advantages of buying office space are that the mortgage interest expense is tax-deductible and you will build equity in the property over time. The disadvantages are that you cannot move out at the end of your lease like a lessee can and you are responsible for maintenance and upkeep on the office space. In addition, if the value of the property goes down or does not appreciate significantly, your equity will not grow and may, in fact, go down.

In many communities it is possible to purchase a house for use as an office for a reasonable price. In larger metropolitan areas, that option may not be as affordable. If you decide to buy and rent space to other lawyers, find out what legal obligations arise from being a landlord. If you plan to remodel an existing building, find out what improvements will be required to bring it up to code and to make it accessible for people with disabilities. At a minimum, be prepared to make the building wheelchair accessible and to improve restroom facilities to accommodate wheelchairs. If planned and executed correctly, buying a building and renting to other lawyers can help you cover your mortgage payment. If not done correctly, being a landlord can be an unpleasant and expensive experience.

Virtual Office

Although you have all those office space options to choose from, there is another option—the "virtual office." A virtual office can be *any* place where you can be in touch with your staff by phone or computer, read your mail online, access your files remotely, create and edit documents, and perform virtually all of the activities associated with running your practice and managing your cases.

Computer technology and the Internet are the keys to creating a virtual office. With fast computers and high-speed Internet access, lawyers can appear to be "in the office" even though they are not really there. Lawyers can easily dial into the office computer from their laptop from a coffee shop near the courthouse. Cases can be reviewed and work can be assigned to support staff without the lawyer being physically present in the office.

If I am planning to be out of the office for a day, I will have my legal assistant scan the day's mail and e-mail it to me directly from our office photocopier as a PDF (Portable Document Format) document. Using Adobe Acrobat software, I can "open the mail" from a coffee shop or another office, enter comments on the letters, motions, or pleadings, then e-mail them back to my assistant for action. This ability has saved me many late-night trips back to the office just to read the mail.

What's more, with video conferencing rapidly becoming an affordable and reliable technology, remote face-to-face communications are becoming more commonplace. Keep these developments in mind when considering the type and amount of physical space your PI practice will require.

Organizing the Law Office

Office space is one of the largest fixed expenses for a personal injury lawyer, so it is important not to pay for any more space than you need. One way to keep costs low is to avoid large offices in favor of smaller offices and a larger conference room for meeting clients and conducting depositions and arbitration hearings. Office costs can also be reduced by storing files off site in a low-cost storage facility (or in the basement of your home at no cost).

Support staff needs are another important consideration. Whether they work at desks in an open area or in individual cubicles or in offices, support personnel should have adequate work areas. For those employees who share a work area with others, provision should be made for a quiet, private space for telephone conversations.

You will also need to consider your legal research needs. In the past many personal injury lawyers had a library full of law books. The lawyer had to buy the books and then pay the publisher for periodic updates. The lawyer also had to dedicate a room to those books and pay rent for that room. Finally, the lawyer needed to pay someone to take the outdated pages from the books and file the updates manually. While many lawyers still use that system, most of what you need can be obtained online.

New PI lawyers will find most of what they need to be available online at a fraction of the cost of buying books and periodicals. If you need to read books, use the local law library or arrange to use another firm's library. As the practice begins to mature and the lawyer begins to develop an interest in a specialized area of law, it may then be appropriate to purchase selected books and CDs. In most states, statutes, regulations, and case law are available online for free or a nominal charge. Exceptions to this rule include books that you use regularly and will take to depositions, arbitration hearings, or trials and include evidence and civil procedure rules.

Computer Hardware and Technology

To build a successful personal injury practice, you must integrate computers and other hardware, software tools, online resources, and other technology. Whether you purchase Windows or Macintosh, the cost of a fast computer with a large hard drive has never been lower. (By the time the next edition of this book comes out, many more of us may be using Linux-based computers, but that is for another book.)

Compared with only a couple of years ago, computers today are many times faster and sell for a fraction of the price. Other peripheral hardware items, such as printers and scanners, also have become more powerful and have declined in price. The cost of networking has decreased so much that many law offices can easily afford to install a network to enable all computer users in the office to communicate by e-mail; to access the Internet; and to share printers, fax machines, and other equipment.

The lawyers who benefit the most from technology are those who use it on a regular basis. Lawyers who still don't have a computer on their desk are quickly going the way of the dinosaurs. Unfortunately, though, in thousands of law offices across the country there are lawyers whose desktop computers go unused most of the time. There are lawyers who have sophisticated calendaring programs on those computers but who prefer to handwrite all of their appointments in a pocket calendar. There are also lawyers who prefer to dictate a form letter or pleading for their secretary to transcribe rather than to call up the form on their own computer screen and fill in the blanks. There are even lawyers who still insist on getting all of their documents back from their secretary in draft form so they can mark them up for retyping rather than editing the documents themselves on the computer screen. Those lawyers will never benefit from technology—and don't care. Don't be like them.

Printers

High-resolution laser printers are inexpensive and make documents look like they came from a print shop. Color printers let you add realism, clarity, and a lot of pizzazz to your settlement brochures.

What's more, you can save money printing your letterhead in the office instead of buying it from a commercial printer.

Photocopiers and Scanners

A decade ago, photocopiers made copies but that's about all they did. Today, photocopiers are an integral part of your office network, and, with the right copier, anyone can send documents directly to the copier and distribute electronic copies without ever seeing a piece of paper.

In many offices, photocopiers have also taken over the function of the office printer, providing laser-quality printing in black and white or color.

Most photocopiers have scanning capability and allow you to output documents as TIFF (Tagged Image Format File) or PDF files. Color scanners are essential for scanning photos of accident scenes, wrecked cars, and people. I typically scan medical records when they arrive and then send them electronically to claims representatives or opposing counsel. It allows me to save both time and expense.

Telephone Equipment and Service

The telephone equipment you will need to open your office includes all the telephones and the box that goes in the closet to hold all the phone lines. You can buy either new or used equipment. Buying new equipment is expensive. Buying used equipment will save you a lot of money and, if you get the equipment from a reputable installer, it may still be under a manufacturer's warranty. Getting phone lines installed involves making a call to a local telephone provider. Most installation work is done by telecom companies rather than by the telephone company that sells you the phone lines.

The local phone company runs its lines into the building and someone else runs the lines into the individual offices. Getting the lines into your office will be your responsibility. It involves physically wiring the lines into the office and connecting those inside lines to the phone company's lines so that you can make and receive calls and all the buttons on your phone set light up correctly. The inside installer can serve as your liaison with the telephone company and save you from spending a lot of time "on hold."

A development since the first edition of this book is the availability of VOIP (voice-over Internet protocol) telephone service, where you place calls through your computer and the calls are routed over data lines rather than traditional telephone lines. VOIP is relatively new and commands a small share of the market, but it is increasing in popularity, primarily because it costs much less than standard voice lines.

In addition to regular phone lines, you will also need high-speed Internet access. Presently, most law offices get Internet access either via DSL (digital subscriber lines) or broadband cable. Not every office can get DSL for technical reasons, but your local telephone provider can tell you whether it is available at your location.

Your inside telephone installer can also advise you regarding options for voice mail, music-on-hold, and other services.

Marketing the Personal Injury Practice **5**

A MARKETING PLAN IS ONLY ONE PART of an overall practice development plan, but it is a vital part. Once you decide what kind of practice you want to build, your marketing plan will provide a road map to help you avoid getting lost along the way. Your marketing plan will include

- ◆ goals (e.g., establish a personal injury practice emphasizing automobile accident claims);
- ◆ strategies (e.g., develop name familiarity in the metropolitan area by opening offices in surrounding suburbs); and
- ◆ tactics (e.g., advertise on area television stations and in the Yellow Pages).

If you need help designing and implementing a marketing plan, hire a consultant to assist you. The consultant can play as large or as small a role as you want and can afford. There are also software programs that will aid you in putting together your marketing plan. (A sample form for drafting an overall marketing plan is provided in Appendix A.)

Many lawyers express a resistance to marketing their services, but the reality is that all lawyers engage in marketing in one way or another. Some do it in a systematic manner with strategies, plans, and tactics, while others market themselves informally without any structured plan. No matter what else you do to build your practice, however, you must let people know that you are a personal injury lawyer and what kinds of cases you handle. We have all cringed when a former client or a friend or acquaintance with an injury claim has said, "I didn't call you because I didn't think that you handled that kind of case." If people don't know what kinds of cases you handle, when will they ever call you for help? Tell everyone that you are a personal injury lawyer and that you handle auto accident cases (if that is what you do). Don't be shy or embarrassed about telling people. If you are determined to pursue this entrepreneurial line of work, you must be willing to promote yourself.

Market Analysis

Market analysis is a critical part of any marketing plan. It includes gathering information on potential clients in the market and on the other lawyers who now serve that market. Personal injury law includes traditional areas such as automobile accidents, premises liability, intentional torts (e.g., assault and battery), products liability, and medical malpractice. However, it also extends beyond such areas into workplace claims for employment discrimination and sexual harassment. These workplace claims have expanded in recent years as a result both of legislative action and judicial decisions. In addition, many successful personal injury lawyers have achieved success and notoriety in handling cases concerning consumer fraud, claims against financial institutions, and securities fraud. In deciding what kinds of cases to handle, lawyers must take only cases that they can handle in a competent and professional manner, but at the same time lawyers must be flexible enough to spot new opportunities for practice growth and professional development.

In analyzing the market it is important to know who is currently serving the market and what it will take to enter and compete for a share of business. Start with the local Yellow Pages and see who is advertising for personal injury cases. Local television stations or advertising agencies can help you identify the biggest lawyer advertisers. Next, check with jury verdict services to see who is appearing in court on personal injury cases. Judges and their staff members also will give you that information.

The High-Volume Market

Every city has a number of well-known, highly visible lawyers who handle a high volume of automobile accident cases and other cases. They can often be found advertising on reruns of "Perry Mason" in the middle of the day. After you find out who they are, you must decide how to enter the market and compete with them for a share of the available business. Marketing experts speak of "barriers to entry" into a particular market that will discourage people from entering that market. Personal injury law is not without its own barriers to entry. The main barrier to entering a high-volume personal injury market is money: money for television advertising, money for Yellow Pages advertising, and money for other advertising. If you have the money to advertise, however, you can enter that market and, unless the market is saturated, you should be able to get a share of the available cases. If the market under consideration is saturated with personal injury lawyers, look at nearby communities for opportunities. Many times communities only a few miles away from a major city will be a completely different market and will present greater opportunities for you to establish yourself. The market analysis sheet provided in Appendix B can help you assess the number of high-volume firms in your area as well as those firms' advertising efforts.

The best market information you can have is the number of new cases that each firm or lawyer opens each year. That information will let you calculate that firm's market share and market rank. Most lawyers probably won't give you that specific information, but they may be willing to talk with you and give you some general information. Call them and ask for an appointment to meet with them. If you manage to get a meeting (or even a telephone conversation), ask the following questions:

◆ How effective are the Yellow Pages in advertising your practice?

- From what geographical area do most of your new calls come?
- How many new calls do you receive every week on average?
- Which TV stations are most effective?
- What trends have you noticed in the market in the past year?
- What changes do you expect in the next year or two?
- What demographics are you targeting?
- What would you do differently if you were just starting a PI practice?

They will be flattered that you asked them rather than one of their competitors. They may be so proud of their success that they tell you everything you want to know. You won't know until you ask.

Getting Referrals from Other Attorneys

The barriers to entry into the more specialized areas of personal injury law are just as formidable as in the high-volume areas and can't be overcome simply by spending a lot of money on advertising. That is because lawyers who handle specialty cases such as medical and legal malpractice claims or products liability claims routinely get most of their cases through referrals from other lawyers. The referring lawyers may themselves be personal injury lawyers, but they prefer to refer these cases to an "expert." You cannot just advertise and expect to get referrals. Unless you have experience in handling malpractice claims, your lack of experience will be a barrier to getting other lawyers to refer those cases to you.

If your goal is to develop a referral-based practice, your time line will need to be much longer than for a high-volume practice. In the beginning, malpractice and products liability cases will make up only a small portion of your caseload, alongside automobile accidents and other cases. As you develop your skills in handling more-complicated cases, you will also develop a reputation and referrals will follow.

Office Location as a Marketing Tool

Most personal injury lawyers don't realize that office location is part of your marketing program. After they decide to open their own practice, they get a few leads on available office space and sign a lease—perhaps without even thinking about how office location will affect whether you get clients, where those clients will come from, and whether the experience of coming to your office will be convenient and satisfying or inconvenient and burdensome.

Especially if your goal is to build a high-volume practice—auto accidents especially—geography should be a critical factor in choosing the location of your office. The reason is that prospective clients are probably not going to be willing to drive a long distance to get to your office when there are other lawyers whose offices are closer to their homes or work. If you plan to build your practice with low-volume, "big ticket" specialized cases such as medical malpractice and products liability, location will be a less-important consideration because more of your cases will probably come from referrals and people will be willing to make more of an effort to see you.

Will locating in a city center be the best option for you? There are advantages to locating in a downtown area. If your practice will require regular court appearances, having an office close to the courthouse will save you travel time, and courthouses are usually located in the city center. Also, downtown offices are usually easier to reach by public transportation than are suburban offices. Another advantage of having a downtown office is that, while it may not be as convenient as other locations, it is centrally located and will allow you to draw people from the city as well as nearby suburbs and towns. In addition, you can draw from the large number of people who commute into the city to work every day. Since they are in the city during business hours, your downtown office would be most convenient for them. Additionally, newer downtown office buildings will be more accessible to clients with disabilities than will offices located in older buildings or converted houses.

For your clients, the disadvantages of your having a downtown office are that transportation and parking may be problems. Many people do not like to go "into the city," especially in large cities. Offer validated parking if you can. In appropriate situations, send a taxi or help the client arrange transportation or go to the client's home for a conference. Providing that kind of help may bring in clients who otherwise would not be willing to hire a "downtown lawyer." Another disadvantage of locating downtown is that the better office space is often more expensive in the city center. Although rents in suburban office buildings also are quite expensive, the lower-rent offices in cities are often less desirable than those in outlying areas.

If you plan to practice in a smaller city or town, location will be less of a consideration. If traffic congestion is not a problem and rents are the same throughout the community, a location near the courthouse will probably be the most convenient for you.

The advantage of locating out of the city center is that your clients won't be inconvenienced by having to go downtown to see you. Yet if you aren't going to locate downtown and your market encompasses a large geographical area, where should you locate? If you know what part of the area your clients will come from, locate your office there. Make it as convenient as possible for your clients to get to your office. Many lawyers whose offices are outside of the downtown core area find success locating near shopping malls. Most malls are well-known landmarks, and they attract shoppers from a great distance away.

My most recent office was in a suburb only a couple of miles away from a chiropractic physician who handled a lot of auto accident cases. He would give those of his new patients who were not represented the names of two or three lawyers. Because I was so close, I got more calls than the lawyers whose offices were located downtown—more than ten miles away.

If your office is located in a building with other tenants, let them know what kinds of cases you handle and ask them for referrals. Many lawyers have gotten referrals from people they know only from the elevator in their office building.

Multiple Offices

In considering whether to have multiple offices, client convenience will be the most important issue. How likely is it that prospective clients who live on the other side of the city will drive across town to get to your office? If you plan to advertise your practice throughout a metropolitan area, is one location going to be enough? If one location won't be enough, consider opening a second office in another part of your market area so that clients will have a choice.

Supporting multiple full-service offices is an expensive and labor-intensive undertaking. A less costly alternative for the lawyer just starting a personal injury practice is to open a branch office but handle all paperwork at the main office. Many lawyers who use the main office-branch office approach locate their branch offices in an "executive suite" with office space, reception, coffee, photocopies, and related services provided. The lawyer has the choice of renting an office full-time or renting an office on a part-time, as-needed basis. A part-time office is less expensive, but the lawyer may have to use a different space on each visit.

Another option is to rent an office from another lawyer or law firm to use as a branch office. An advantage of opening a low-cost branch office is that you can close it or move it if it doesn't turn out to be productive. Often lawyers will have one or more extra offices that are available for rent as a branch office. The best lawyer to rent from is one who practices in a different area of law and who will refer personal injury cases to you. You, in return, can refer appropriate cases to that lawyer.

Differentiation

Differentiation is the process of distinguishing yourself from the competition. It involves giving prospective clients a reason to call you rather than some other lawyer. Personal injury lawyers, unlike businesses selling a product, do not differentiate based on price. Yellow Pages publishers have traditionally not allowed lawyers to include information on pricing. Personal injury lawyers, unlike soft-drink manufacturers, cannot differentiate based on comparisons with the competition. Some lawyers have successfully distinguished themselves based on the kinds of cases they handle (e.g., "Auto Accidents Only") or their convenient location, and others have emphasized service (e.g., "House Calls, Evening, and Weekend Appointments"). From the kind of marketing that they engage in, however, it would appear that most lawyers don't attempt to differentiate themselves at all. Those lawyers who do make that attempt will stand out from the rest of the crowd. Appendix C contains a worksheet to help you identify positive ways in which you differ from the competition.

One way to differentiate yourself from the competition is by targeting prospective clients whose primary language is one other than English. People whose primary language is Spanish, in particular, make up an increasing percentage of every state as more and more people come here from Spanish-speaking countries. Immigration from Eastern Europe, from the former Soviet Union, and from Asian countries has led to an increase in the need for lawyers who can speak and write (or have staff who can speak and write) Russian, Chinese, Vietnamese, and other languages that may not have been offered when we went to high school. In some cases, people from these countries speak no English at all, and in other cases, they speak some English, but prefer to speak their native language when discussing complicated legal matters. Unfortunately, too few lawyers are able to converse in languages other than English or have staff who speak a range of foreign languages. Expanding the number of languages spoken at your office will help you expand your practice quickly!

For several years I had an ad in the local "Spanish Yellow Pages." At the time, it cost a fraction of the main Yellow Pages directory. The book was distributed in targeted communities and was available at markets, stores, doctors' offices, and other places in the Spanish-speaking community. The results were phenomenal, but the cases took extra time because of the language issue. There are specialized directories in most communities that target particular segments of the non-English speaking population. They are usually a good value and result in a lot of calls.

Another way to differentiate yourself is to target other specialized groups. One colleague of mine has built a practice on his bicycling hobby—he advertises himself as the advocate for bicyclists who have been hit by careless motorists. Another colleague, an avid motorcyclist, has done the same with that audience.

Marketing Strategies and Tactics

Once you have analyzed the market and decided how you will enter it and differentiate yourself from the competition, your task will be to communicate who you are, what you do, and why people should call you. You will want to communicate with the following groups:

- People who have been injured in the past and have not resolved their claims
- People who may become injured in the future
- Friends and family of those people who have been injured and who may recommend a lawyer to the injured person
- Professionals who come in contact with injured persons and who may be in a position to recommend a lawyer
- Lawyers who do not handle PI cases and who may be in a position to recommend a lawyer who handles such cases
- Lawyers who handle PI cases but who want to bring in another lawyer to help with a particular case

How will you communicate with all these groups? Here are some common but effective tools.

Business Cards—The Basic Marketing Tool

If you are like most lawyers, you hand out hundreds of business cards every year. In many cases, people will put your card away and forget who you are. When they find your card later on, will it tell them who you are and what you do? Does it say "Attorney-at-Law," or does it say "Personal Injury Lawyer: Handling auto accidents, medical malpractice, products liability, and workers' compensation cases"? Which card tells your story the most effectively?

Business cards are inexpensive and easy to produce. You can use any word processing or page layout program to design a business card on your computer today, e-mail the file to Kinko's or some other print shop, and pick the cards up in a few days.

Brochures

Law firm brochures range from the simple and inexpensive to the elaborate and very expensive. They can be as simple as a tri-folded 8 1/2-by-11-inch sheet of paper or as elaborate as a small catalog.

Brochures provide a forum for saying everything that you want to about yourself and your practice. Ideally, the recipient will read the brochure and keep it for future reference. Be sure that it looks like a document worth keeping and not something to be tossed out with the junk mail.

Brochures help the personal injury lawyer deal with a serious problem that all lawyers have—people forget your name. It is common for clients who have two accident claims in a short time to use a different lawyer for the second claim because they forgot the name of their first lawyer. Marketing involves communication and brochures are an effective way to communicate your availability. A brochure is just one more way to remind prospective clients that you are there to help them when they need you.

A brochure about your personal injury practice should be written for non-lawyers and should be written in a different style than one directed toward a prospective business client. Prospective personal injury clients want to know what kinds of cases you handle, where your office is located, and whether they can see you at night or on weekends. They also want to know whether you will take their case on a contingency basis. In short, your brochure needs to speak for you and answer the client's questions.

Since most word processing programs have page-layout features, including graphics capabilities, you or your staff can create a brochure with little professional assistance. You might, however, want to consult a graphic artist for layout ideas or a copywriter for help in delivering your message. Even if you hire some design help, most of the expense of preparing a brochure will still be in the printing costs. Most small-firm brochures are tri-folded 8 1/2-by-11-inch pages and are not expensive to produce. Your local printer can advise you about the best paper stock to use and about using colors effectively. Remember, a brochure is not simply a resume. It is an advertisement, and it should have a theme and convey a message just like any other advertisement.

Once you have produced your brochure, you will want to distribute it as widely as possible. Start with your current and former clients. (If you don't have any current or former clients, send your brochure to friends and relatives, business associates, fraternity or sorority members, church members, parents of your children's classmates, etc.)

Former clients will welcome a personal letter from you, with your brochure and business card enclosed, reminding them that you haven't forgotten them and that you are available to help them with their legal problems if the need should ever arise. Invite them to call for a free consultation if they have a problem. Let them know that you are available and accessible. Don't be timid about asking them to refer their friends and family to you. You will find that most people take pride in referring others to *their* lawyer. Don't forget to send a thank-you letter to clients who refer their friends or family members to you.

Without the brochure or any follow-up on your part, it won't be long before former clients no longer think of you as their lawyer. Worse yet, they often forget the name of their former lawyer entirely and start over with someone new when they next need some legal help.

Your current clients are a fertile ground for marketing—both in terms of getting other work from the same clients and of getting referrals from them. Often a client has more than one legal matter going on at the same time. Many times people will go to one lawyer for a workers' compensation claim and to another lawyer for a medical malpractice claim, thinking that the first lawyer only handles workers' compensation claims. Your brochure will give your clients a clear picture of what kinds of cases you handle and let them know that you would welcome their calls as well as calls from their friends and family. Give several of your brochures to every new client you meet, whether you take their case or not. Often when you meet prospective clients, you spend your time talking about the problem that has brought them to your office and you do not discuss the other kinds of cases that you handle. Send them a follow-up letter a week or so after that first meeting, thanking them for consulting you and enclosing your brochure.

Other prospective clients that are often overlooked, and to whom your brochure should be sent, are people who have called you or come in for advice in the past but haven't become clients. Be sure to keep them on your mailing list and let them know that even though you were not able to help them with their present problem, they should call you if they need a lawyer in the future. When you consider what you spend in time and money to get total strangers to call you with their legal problems, it is a bargain to send a follow-up letter and brochure to them when they do call. If you have treated them with courtesy and made a good impression during your meeting or phone conversation, your brochure and letter will reinforce that impression and increase the chance of their calling you the next time they need a lawyer. When they call again, it may be concerning a legal problem that you do not handle. In that case, you can help them find someone who can help them. They will be impressed with your thoughtfulness and the lawyer you find will be appreciative, as well.

Newsletters

Many lawyers use newsletters to keep in touch with clients. The information in the newsletters may relate strictly to insurance and personal injury topics, or it may be more general in nature. Newsletters are an excellent vehicle for advising clients and others on changes in state or federal laws and other important issues such as tort reform.

Some lawyers and law firms use the newsletter to discuss cases that they have worked on and results that they have achieved for their clients. Others use the newsletter as a firm brochure with information about individual lawyers and their qualifications. Still others fill their newsletters with topical information about particular types of cases so that readers can learn about their legal rights and options. As with other forms of advertising, some newsletters are subtle and understated, while others are direct and bold solicitations.

Individual lawyers' newsletters can also be an important part of political campaigns undertaken by state or national trial lawyers' organizations to urge the passing or defeat of legislation that will impact the rights of citizens to seek remedies when they are injured. Lawyers can purchase newsletters for distribution to their clients from national companies that produce the publications and print the lawyer's or law firm's name on them.

Newsletters can be printed for use as handouts in the office; mailed to a distribution list; e-mailed in electronic format (PDF or word processing files); or posted on your Web site.

Examples of personal injury lawyers who have newsletters available on their Web sites can be found by searching the Web.

Bar and CLE Activities

Participating in bar association activities is an effective way to get to know other lawyers and to get name recognition in the legal community. Lawyers usually get a great deal of satisfaction from participating on bar committees, and it is something that you may have a professional obligation to do, but it is not generally an effective tool in building a personal injury practice. Lawyers develop reputations in a variety of ways and being active in the bar is a good way to develop a reputation for being interested in such things as pro bono, legal services for the poor, bar admissions, or continuing legal education activities. However, if you want to develop a reputation for being a good personal injury lawyer, one who is worthy of being referred cases, you should strive to achieve that reputation. The best way to achieve that reputation, quite frankly, is by having success in the courtroom or settling some high-profile cases. In addition, you can achieve a reputation as a PI lawyer by being active in bar activities that involve issues important to other PI lawyers. Here are some ways that you can get involved.

- ◆ Join the Association of Trial Lawyers of America (ATLA) and your state trial lawyers' association and become involved in their sections and committees.
- ◆ Join the litigation or personal injury sections of your state and local bar associations.
- ◆ Join the American Bar Association and the Law Practice Management Section.
- ◆ Attend conventions and meetings of those organizations and volunteer to organize future meetings.
- ◆ Volunteer to edit or write for a newsletter featuring issues of interest to personal injury lawyers.
- ◆ Volunteer to organize or speak at future continuing legal education (CLE) programs.

While most CLE programs are sponsored by bar organizations, many such programs are sponsored by private entities, both for-profit and not-for-profit, and they are usually looking for new speakers. The higher-profile and more-prestigious CLE programs at trial lawyer conventions and meetings are the exclusive province of the lawyers who appear regularly and tell stories about their most recent big verdicts. Don't expect to break into those programs. The best opportunity to get onto a CLE panel is when you can talk about a specialized topic such as tort reform, new legislation, new court rules, changes in the evidence code, recent court decisions, and other topics that can be learned and presented by someone who has never gotten a million-dollar verdict. If you do a good job, you may be invited back to speak again.

If you are going to spend the time that it takes to work your way up in a bar organization, the local trial lawyers' association is a good place to do it. At the same time that you are building your reputation as a personal injury lawyer, you will be meeting and learning from more experienced lawyers. Don't be intimidated if some of them have "been there, done that" attitudes. There are many trial lawyers who have not forgotten how hard it was when they were young and inexperienced and who will take the time to give you advice on how to build your practice. Many trial lawyers' associations have formal mentoring programs in which experienced lawyers are paired with new lawyers for a year or two.

Advertising

Advertising is a far less controversial topic than it once was. While some lawyers, particularly older lawyers, continue to oppose advertising on the grounds that it is unprofessional, surveys conducted by the American Bar Association Commission on Advertising show that the public does not share those lawyers' views. Twenty years ago, few professionals advertised. Now, it seems as though ads and commercials for doctors (especially those who do plastic surgery and vision correction) are as common as those for lawyers.

Advertising is the one way in which young lawyers can compete with established firms for clients. Advertising has given new lawyers a fighting chance to get cases that would traditionally have gone to the big firms. It has definitely leveled the playing field.

Lawyer advertising began with personal injury lawyers, and personal injury lawyers remain the biggest advertisers. Television commercials for PI lawyers have long been a staple of daytime and late-night television. Yellow Pages ads for lawyers now include two-page ads, five-color spreads, and specialty guides. According to the ABA Commission, the public regards the Yellow Pages as an effective place to find a PI lawyer. PI lawyers advertise because it is an effective way to reach a large number of potential clients, but also because they feel that they have to advertise to compete with other lawyers. One firm calls its advertising program "defensive advertising" because it knows it would fall behind the competition if it didn't advertise.

The Yellow Pages

Most personal injury lawyers who decide to advertise start with an ad in a local Yellow Pages directory. It is probably the most effective thing that they could do. When I started my practice in 1980, our city had one Yellow Pages directory, and it was published by the local telephone company. Now there are numerous directories (and it is difficult to say who the phone company is anymore). The Yellow Pages (whichever book you are talking about) contains hundreds of display ads for lawyers, ranging from a one-inch column ad to two or more full pages. Directories often have advertising on the front and back pages and down the spine. Many directories have online versions for shoppers who prefer to find lawyers that way.

Why should a lawyer advertise in the Yellow Pages? Because people still look there when they need a lawyer. That's a good reason, in my opinion. If you regularly ask new clients how they came to call you and the answer is always that "I found you in the Yellow Pages," you begin to get the message.

Once you have decided to put your "toe in the water" with Yellow Pages advertising, you have to decide on which directory to advertise in and what size ad to buy. Yellow Pages advertisements are normally put in the book in order of size, according to seniority among ads of that size. The largest ads are always first in each section and the most senior advertisers are in the front of each section. For example, if you purchase a half-page ad, it will appear at the end of the half-page ads if yours is the newest ad in that size. However, your half-page ad will still appear ahead of the quarter-page ads, regardless of their seniority in the book. So, if you want to be in the front of the book rather than in the back, you will have to buy a larger and more expensive ad. Most lawyers prefer to be in the front of the book. One lawyer asked a caller why she had picked him out of all the lawyers in the Yellow Pages. The caller responded that she figured that if the lawyer could afford the cost of a large ad, he must be doing well in his practice and she wanted a successful lawyer to handle her case. It is true that it takes more effort to page through the book and get to the smaller ads in the back. Callers are more likely to start at the front and page through the book until an ad catches their attention.

One way to test the cost-effectiveness of your Yellow Pages advertising is to use a different telephone number in each ad. That way, you can track the exact number of calls generated by each advertisement.

Most Yellow Pages books are formatted so that the regular lawyer ads are followed by "guides," or ads for different specialty areas, also called "areas of concentration" (for states that do not recognize or certify specialization), arranged alphabetically. The main category of interest to the personal injury lawyer will be called "Accidents and Personal Injuries" (normally the first category listed alphabetically in the specialty guides). This is usually the largest specialty area for PI lawyers, but other categories include "Medical Malpractice" (or "Professional Negligence"), "Defective Products," and "Accidents/Property Damage." Some Yellow Pages publishers sell large display ads in the specialty guides, while others sell only in-column ads or plain listings in the guides.

Your Yellow Pages Ad

In their excellent book, *The Lawyer's Guide to Effective Yellow Pages Advertising,* Second Edition, (American Bar Association, Law Practice Management Section, 2005), authors Kerry Randall and Andru Johnson observe that:

> Advertising in the Yellow Pages is unlike advertising anywhere else. Your Yellow Pages ad must be constructed specifically for the Yellow Pages or it won't work—it just won't attract calls from the potential clients you want to see. Advertisers who do not understand the uniqueness of the Yellow Pages medium do not get powerful results with their Yellow Pages advertising.

The authors say that "Yellow Pages advertising is different enough to be a spotted zebra" and that two of the zebra's spots are content orientation and "wants-based versus needs-based buying."

Randall and Johnson explain that when someone opens a Yellow Pages book, that person has "already decided to make a purchase" and is "now looking for direction to make the purchase." For that reason, they explain, some "rules" about advertising do not apply to Yellow Pages advertising.

The book sets out a step-by-step approach to creating the "best ad in the directory." That approach will result in "transforming a good ad into a powerful ad."

The six key elements of high-performing ads, according to Randall and Johnson are

1. strong headlines that command attention and engage readers;
2. a laser-sharp focus; a willingness to ignore most readers;
3. arresting, eye-captivating illustrations or photographs;
4. clearly identifiable differences (from competitive advertisers);
5. relevant copy (text) that covers less than 50 percent of the ad space; and
6. professional-looking, clutter-free layouts.

The Lawyer's Guide to Effective Yellow Pages Advertising, Second Edition (American Bar Association, 2005), includes advice on designing your ad (and getting the help you need to do it right), advice on developing powerful emotional content, and advice on deciding whether your ad should "talk to women or men." The book gives examples of good ads and bad ads. (I will admit to recognizing some of my ads in the latter category.)

According to the authors, if you follow their advice, "you will be getting the calls your competitors dream about." What more could anyone want?

Yellow Pages ads cost money—often a lot of money. The price of an ad will depend on its size and whether or not it contains color. To make your advertisement stand out, you can add color, for an extra charge, of course. Is the extra color worth the price? It depends on whom you ask. Some sales representatives and consultants will tell you that a smaller ad with lots of color is more attractive to consumers than is a large ad done in black ink on the standard yellow background. Which is more important, color or ad size? Will users thumb through the large ads to find your small ad, or will they stop with the large ads and never get to see your colorful ad? If success is any measure of the effectiveness of advertising, it seems that most of the "big name" personal injury lawyers who advertise in the Yellow Pages make liberal use of color and also have big ads. Does that mean that you should buy a big ad with lots of color? It is difficult to say whether the Yellow Pages brought successful lawyers their success or whether their success allows them to pay for the big ads.

My twenty-plus years of experience tells me that if you have to choose between a large ad or color, choose the large ad to get to the front of the book. If you have to choose between an ad in the guides and an ad in the general lawyer section, choose the one that puts you closest to the front of the book.

Randall and Johnson put it another way. Their view is that "the more the ad costs, the greater the opportunity the advertiser has." The authors wisely suggest that "you must evaluate color, white knockouts, and other features from an inquiry into how each dollar can generate the greatest revenue." Better yet, they tell you how to do that evaluation.

Which Yellow Pages Book?

Once you have decided to advertise in the Yellow Pages, you must next decide which book or books to advertise in. Most metropolitan areas have a main telephone book with Yellow Pages and one or more suburban directories with their own Yellow Pages. If you advertise in one or more of the suburban books, your budget can double or triple easily. Most publishers do not offer quantity discounts for ads in multiple books, although occasionally they do offer special prices to entice advertisers to increase the size of their ads or expand into a new book. When it comes time to renew, however, the "regular rates" apply and the teaser discounts go away. They hope that by then you will either be pleased with the results or afraid to take your ad out of the book even if the results have not been successful.

Yellow Pages publishers will present you with data to show that their particular book is the most used book in any given area, city, or suburb. View such data carefully. If you have to choose between phone books, pick the biggest one in your area. Selectively go into the smaller books as you can afford to do so.

Advice on Yellow Pages advertisements is available from several sources. The sales representatives for the various Yellow Pages publishers will usually encourage you to purchase the largest ad that you can. Independent advertising consultants will sometimes counsel you to place a smaller ad in the Yellow Pages and to use the difference in cost to advertise in other places. Some companies specialize in "redesigning" your Yellow Pages ad. These firms usually contact you directly by telephone or fax to tell you how poorly designed your ad is. They will charge you a fee to redo the layout of your ad. Other advice can be obtained from advertising consultants who charge on an hourly basis and have no vested interest in selling advertising to you. I recommend this option. In any case, the lawyer starting out in Yellow Pages advertising should be prepared for serious sticker shock. It is easy to get talked into exceeding your budget.

Lawyers' Yellow Pages ads are as diverse as the lawyers who run them. All too often, however, they are filled with graphic cliches (e.g., the scales of justice or eagles flying) and, like many firm brochures, they look like they were designed by a committee (of lawyers). Sometimes small things in ads can put people off. For example, one advertisement contained a photograph of two male lawyers sitting at a table with two female staff members standing behind them. The lawyers were identified by their first and last names, but the women were identified only by their first names. The lawyers reported that they got several comments saying that the ad was demeaning to the women. If that ad had been reviewed by a professional before it went into the book, such a mistake could have been corrected. That is the biggest problem with Yellow Pages mistakes—they last a long time. When you make a mistake in your ad layout or copy, it cannot be corrected for a full year. If your ad is well done and attractive, you will reap the benefits for twelve months. If your ad is dull and ineffective (or even offensive), that year will seem like an eternity. The best advice is to consult a graphic artist or copywriter or some other communications professional. This is not to say that you shouldn't have input in the design of the ad, but you should not be the only person working on it.

In designing your ad, emphasize your strengths. If you have a unique capability to handle certain kinds of personal injury cases, be sure to say so. If you have a nurse or other medical personnel on staff, include that fact as well. If you have multiple offices or convenient hours, your readers will surely want to be informed of that.

Put your e-mail address and Web site link in your ad, and invite readers to send questions to you by e-mail.

One final suggestion is that you take the time to have your ad printed long before the Yellow Pages deadline and then convene a focus group to look at it and tell you what they like or dislike about it. Ask them to compare your ad to others that they like more or less and to tell you why. It will be worth your time and effort.

Television Advertising

Television advertising is what separates the committed from the timid in personal injury law. TV commercials cost a lot of money.

Television advertising is generally local, except for commercials by law firms who advertise for class action or mass-tort plaintiffs in cases involving defective pharmaceutical products and the like.

With television commercials being very expensive and television advertising relying heavily on the science of demographics, you would be well served by consulting an advertising agency before venturing alone into these waters. For the most part, the television station pays a commission to the ad agency, so it will not cost you any more than the cost of producing and running the commercials. You have two options for your commercial. The first is to purchase a ready-made commercial and insert your name at the end. These "canned" commercials are sold to law firms in different television markets throughout the country. These commercials usually feature a spokesperson with a look of authority telling viewers why they need to have a lawyer and why they should call the lawyer running the commercial. The themes for these ads include "No recovery—no fee," "Don't get hurt twice by not having a lawyer," "We'll help you with your medical bills and lost income," "You need someone in your corner," and so on. The advantage of purchasing these commercials is that the companies that produce and sell them have done the market research and know what should appeal to viewers. The disadvantage is that they tend to be fairly expensive and impersonal, with your name appearing only at the beginning and end of the commercial.

For those lawyers bold enough to venture personally onto the airwaves, most TV stations and advertising agencies can recommend someone who can produce a commercial for you. The producer's job is to write the script and plan the shots in advance, then shoot the commercial, and later add "voice-over" sound and edit the entire project down to a thirty-second commercial. Many personal injury lawyers like to appear in their own commercials, thinking that the public wants to know whom they are dealing with when they call. Many clients see a commercial without remembering the name of the lawyer but then go to the Yellow Pages and select the lawyer whose face they saw on TV.

The disadvantage of producing your own commercial is that economic considerations might result in a commercial that looks and sounds "low budget." We have all seen commercials on local stations that look like they were shot on a shoestring budget. Keep in mind that the public is used to watching television and they are used to seeing high-quality, professionally done, entertaining commercials. If your commercial looks unprofessional, the viewer may see you and your firm as unprofessional as well, and your message may be lost in the process.

Before appearing in your own commercial, you should give yourself a "screen test" and ask others to tell you how you come across on the small screen. You may be attractive, charming, and eloquent in real life, but that does not guarantee that you will look good on television. TV commercials involve acting, and you need to be able to deliver your lines as well as a professional actor to have any credibility with the audience. You do not want viewers to be put off by your presentation.

Different states and jurisdictions have different laws regulating lawyer advertising. Some states restrict the use of paid actors, reenactments, testimonials, and other things that sometimes appear in commercials. Be sure to check your state's regulations before producing or purchasing a television commercial.

Internet Marketing and Advertising

When the first edition of this book was published in 1997, few lawyers had Web sites, Web search engines were in their infancy, and no one with a Web site was concerned about how to drive traffic to that site. Lawyer Web pages were basically online resumes. With the proliferation of Web sites, lawyers, especially personal injury lawyers, cannot simply create Web sites telling prospective clients who they are, where they are, and how they can help them. PI lawyers, at least those who know how the World Wide Web really works, must be very concerned about driving traffic to their Web sites.

In addition to Web sites, lawyers are increasingly using Weblogs (or blogs). Blogs differ from lawyer Web sites in that they are usually updated with new information of interest to readers more often than Web sites. Diligent lawyer-bloggers often post new information daily or weekly. Blogs are easy to read because new postings typically appear at the top of the page. Once you find a blog that catches your attention, you can sign up to be notified by e-mail when new postings are made. If you want to become a blogger, you will find free tools on the Web to make your job easy.

Two good places to get information on legal blogs (sometimes called "blawgs") are *http://www.blawg.org* and *http://law-library .rutgers.edu/resources/lawblogs.html.*

Once you have created a Web site or blog, you will want to drive traffic to your site. The naïve assume that all Web sites are created equal and will be treated equally by the Web search engines and Web directories. Google is the largest search engine. Microsoft has its own search capabilities as part of MSN.com. Yahoo! is a popular resource, but it is a Web directory and not a true search engine. When someone goes to either Google or MSN or Yahoo! or any other search engine or directory and types in the terms "Personal Injury+Lawyer+Philadelphia," you might think that he or she will get a random list of PI lawyers in that city. That is not how it works, though. Some lawyers in Philadelphia are going to get more traffic than others because they have paid to have their Web sites listed ahead of others when certain search terms are entered.

An industry has sprung up in the last decade to help lawyers and other Web advertisers get "more hits" or more visits. Lawyers can get better listings for free by learning more about how companies such as Google and Yahoo! work. The term for making your Web site more desirable for search engines or Web directories is called "Search Engine Optimization." (Take a minute and do a search on "search engine optimization" and you will see what I mean.) Search engine optimization involves the design of your Web site, the selection of the words that appear on the pages (and the words that appear behind the scenes in what are called "metatags"), and the actual coding of the Web pages. Search engines such as Google use software robots, called "spiders," to search the Web on a regular basis to generate lists of words found on Web pages and create indexes of those words and the Web pages on which they were found. The search engine then matches keywords with Web pages and creates "search listings."

Your first task is to design a good Web site, with Web pages that will attract the attention of the spiders. Search engine optimization involves designing Web pages so that the spiders will find the words on your Web pages and include your site on the indexes so that when someone types in one of your keywords or phrases—for example, "Personal Injury Lawyer Philadelphia"—your site will be listed in the search results.

The first generation of lawyers' Web sites was little more than firm brochures. Because of ethical concerns, lawyers were understandably reluctant to put too much information online. Today, effective Web sites will contain valuable content related to the kind of services that you provide. Potential clients may search on specific terms related to their cases and if your Web site does not contain references to those terms, they will never find your Web site. Web site design and maintenance is affordable. You would be well advised to hire an experienced Web site designer to help you with your site. The better Web sites for personal injury lawyers have newsletters that can be downloaded instantly by visitors to the site.

Lawyers who want to catch the attention of the major search engines can pay for placement. Google calls its placement program "AdWords" and says the following on its Web site: "Reach people when they are actively looking for information about your products and services online, and send targeted visitors directly to what you are offering. With AdWords cost-per-click pricing, it's easy to control costs—and you only pay when people click on your ad." Yahoo! calls its program "Sponsored Search." Both companies use a bidding process with the highest bidder for a particular keyword getting the highest placement in the search listings. These are also known as "pay-per-click" programs.

Advertisers bid what they are willing to pay for each click through. A click through occurs when someone sees your name on the search listings on Google, Yahoo!, or somewhere else and then clicks through to your Web site.

Some pay-per-click programs can be as expensive as Yellow Pages advertising. Most online advertising programs will give you an estimate of expected clicks and the total daily projected costs during the bidding process. The good news about Web advertising as compared with the Yellow Pages is that you can quit whenever you want. If you are spending more than you want on clicks, but are not getting any results, you can "turn off" your advertising and come back later, perhaps with different keywords.

Lawyer Referral Services

Private Lawyer Referral Programs

There are many national and regional lawyer referral businesses that run commercials on television. The viewer is encouraged to call a toll-free telephone number and an operator will refer them to a personal injury lawyer in their city. Lawyers pay the referral service to participate in the referral program. Costs usually include a one-time fee, plus ongoing monthly fees. Some referral programs limit the number of participating lawyers within one city, and some even limit the number of lawyers within a zip code or other, smaller geographical designation. Participating lawyers get television advertising without having to pay the costs of producing a commercial or purchasing commercial time on a television station. Some lawyers also like this arrangement because they don't want to be openly associated with advertising, but at the same time want to reap the benefits.

Before signing up for any private lawyer referral program, contact other lawyers who have done so. Speak with them about the number of calls that they have received and about the number of new clients that they have obtained. Find out how well they think the program has paid off for their practice.

Bar-Sponsored Referral Programs

Many state and local bar associations operate lawyer referral programs. Prospective personal injury clients call these programs when they need a lawyer, and the referral program will give them the names of several lawyers who agree to see the client for a reduced fee. Lawyers pay an annual fee to participate in the program, but the fees are usually nominal, often less than one hundred dollars per year. These bar-sponsored programs sometimes advertise on television or radio, but not with the frequency of the private referral programs. Still, because the cost is so low, the lawyer just starting out in practice should definitely sign up.

Newspaper Advertisements

Display advertisements in daily newspapers are not common marketing tools for personal injury lawyers. Some firms have used newspapers to solicit specialized cases involving a large number of claimants, such as, for example, in breast implant cases. Among the reasons that newspaper ads are not more commonly used is that they are expensive and are not targeted at a particular market segment. No lawyer would turn down an offer of a free ad on the front page of a newspaper. However, since newspaper ads are not free, a lawyer choosing this route must decide how often to advertise, what size of ad to run, and what section in which to run the ad. The likelihood that clients who need a PI lawyer will read the newspaper on the day in which the lawyer's ad appears, actually see the ad, and then call the lawyer before the newspaper is dumped into the recycling bin is too small to entice the average PI lawyer.

A form of newspaper advertising that has some appeal for the PI lawyer is the legal question-and-answer column, sometimes known as "Ask a Lawyer." These ads usually run one or two days each week with a number of lawyers in different specialties rotating in and out of the schedule. Most columns tend to contain a number of questions and answers that are recycled regularly. They include such standard questions as: "Who pays my wage loss and medical bills if I've been in an accident?" or "What are my rights if

I am injured by an uninsured motorist?" or "How is compensation for pain and suffering calculated?" Normally the lawyer gives a general answer and invites the questioner to call his or her office for more information (and an appointment, presumably).

Sponsorships

Many large, business-oriented law firms sponsor such things as public television programs, local theater productions, and major civic events. Small personal injury firms cannot afford the cost of such sponsorships, but they can afford to sponsor other community activities. Most communities have activities ranging from softball leagues to free legal clinics to park cleanups for which they solicit sponsors. Other communities have minor league baseball, ice hockey, and other professional sports that offer reasonably priced opportunities for sponsorship.

When considering sponsorships for marketing purposes, be sure to look carefully at the activity and at the demographics of the people who will be involved in or affected by the activity before committing your resources. If the activity does not reach the people you want to attract as clients, your sponsorship dollars will not be well spent. For example, if your prospective clients are mostly hockey fans, your sponsorship of the opera may not make business sense.

Referrals from Other Lawyers

Referrals are the best way to get new clients—and the least expensive. As a general rule, lawyers refer cases to other lawyers they know. As a personal injury lawyer, you should get to know other lawyers and give them a reason to refer PI cases to you. You can begin that relationship by referring non-PI cases to other lawyers and encouraging them to reciprocate.

So if people ask you to handle a business law matter or estate planning case, don't just turn them away—help them find a lawyer who can handle their cases. By helping them, you become their contact person in the mysterious legal world. If they ever need help with a personal injury case, they will naturally call you. Plus, if anyone ever asks them for a referral to a lawyer in a personal injury case, they will give them your name. People enjoy referring friends to their lawyer.

By referring a client to another lawyer, you will generate good will that may result in referrals in the future. Try not to refer clients to lawyers who also handle personal injury cases because they won't ever have any cases to refer to you. When you do refer a client to another lawyer, call the lawyer directly and tell him or her that you are referring a client. Explain that you handle only personal injury cases and that you are helping a client find a lawyer to help with another matter. Find out if that lawyer handles PI cases and, if not, ask the lawyer to consider referring such cases to you. If your jurisdiction allows referral fees, discuss that issue as well. Finally, follow up the call with a letter confirming the conversation and reminding the lawyer that you are available to help his or her clients with personal injury cases. Send some of your business cards and brochures so that the lawyer can give them directly to clients.

If you ask a lawyer to refer a client to you for a specific personal injury matter, be sure to let the lawyer know that you won't "steal" the client or steer the client to a different lawyer for future non-PI problems. Explain that if the client calls you on a subsequent matter, you will advise the client to call the referring lawyer. In addition, always send a thank-you letter to anyone who refers a client to you. (A sample thank-you letter is included in Appendix J, along with other sample letters that you will find helpful in your personal injury practice.)

A good referral source can be other personal injury lawyers who only handle specialized cases, such as medical malpractice or personal injury. Often when lawyers become specialized (or become successful), they are not interested in "garden variety" personal injury cases. Chances are, if you are just starting out, garden-variety cases will be all that you get. Don't be hesitant to ask the "big hitters" in your community to send you their car wrecks and slip and fall cases.

Referrals from Friends

The five largest cases I have settled in my twenty-five year career have all involved personal friends or referrals from personal friends. If your friends do not know what you do for a living, you are missing some great referral opportunities.

Public Relations

A public relations program is a part of a marketing program and, if done effectively, will reinforce your paid advertising efforts. Television and radio stations, as well as newspapers and magazines, regularly use lawyers as sources of information on such issues as legislation, court decisions, and trials of notoriety. In addition, newspapers and magazines regularly publish articles written by lawyers on subjects of interest to their readers. One of the goals of your public relations effort should be to become such a source of information and to get articles published.

If your public relations efforts are successful, you will be the lawyer that the television reporter calls when he or she needs a comment from a lawyer. Eventually, you might be asked to comment "on the air" about issues of the day. Since most people watch television, your prospective clients will see you on TV and think of you as an expert. Even if they don't remember your name right away, when they go to look for a lawyer and see your picture in the Yellow Pages, they may remember seeing you on TV and call you for advice.

You can also get "free media" by issuing a press release when you move your office, add a partner, publish a book or article, or get appointed to a committee or board or commission. Be sure to include your photograph with the press release.

In his chapter entitled "Successful Marketing for the Sole Practitioner" in *Flying Solo: A Survival Guide for the Solo and Small Firm Lawyer,* Fourth Edition, Thomas E. Kane writes that it is a myth that effective marketing is expensive and that large firm lawyers enjoy an advantage over small firm lawyers and solos (a category that includes most personal injury lawyers).

Thomas Kane advises that your marketing/public relations effort should include such activities as arranging speaking engagements, writing, maintaining media contacts, and networking. Kane encourages lawyers to "get to know the local media, whether they are involved in daily, business or legal publications" so that reporters can call on those lawyers when they need a "lawyer's perspective" on an item of current interest. He also suggests approaching a local newspaper about writing a legal column.

I would add that there are benefits from regular online publishing, whether it is on your Web site, blog, or in an online newsletter. Compared to costly print publishing, the Internet provides a free and easy way to get your opinions and viewpoints known, as well as your credentials and expertise. Reporters and editors will now often search the Web for experts rather than "calling around." If they find your Web site or blog, you will have instant credibility. If you are an expert who happens to live in their city or town, you will be the first person they call.

For example, a colleague of mine has had success recently suing doctors who commit malpractice while performing surgery to improve people's eyesight. He now writes regularly and speaks to hospitals, medical associations, and insurance companies about ways to reduce the risk of such surgeries. The publicity that he has generated through his public relations efforts has resulted in increased demand for his services by people who have been the victim of malpractice.

Your Support Staff as Marketers

Your support staff (if you have any) should be enlisted as full-fledged members of your marketing team. Why? Because your secretary, your legal assistant, your bookkeeper, and others who work for you (as employees or contractors) may meet people who need a personal injury lawyer and can refer those people to you. One important point here is that you must have the confidence of your support staff so that they will refer prospective clients to you. I have actually heard other lawyers' secretaries comment that they would never refer someone to their boss because of his (a) personality, (b) sloppy work habits, or (c) inattentiveness to clients' needs, such as never returning telephone calls.

That means that if you are not someone who is easy to work for, considerate of your staff and clients, has good work habits and good ethics, and gives your all to your client's cases, your staff will probably send their friends and acquaintances to your competitors. That is a sad, but true reality.

If you enjoy the support of your staff (and the staff of non-PI lawyers with whom you share office space), make sure that they have your business cards to give to prospective clients. When they refer someone to you, whether you take the case or not, acknowledge their effort and reward them by taking them to lunch or dinner (or better yet, by paying for them to have dinner without you), or by giving them tickets to a sporting event or a concert. If they refer a case that turns out well, your acknowledgment should reflect the success of the case. If they refer a case to you and you settle it and earn a large fee without acknowledging their contribution, I can guarantee that it will be the last time they ever give out your name.

Your Road Map

It is critically important to have a marketing plan in place before you embark on setting up a personal injury practice. You cannot reach your destination without a road map and the marketing plan is your road map. Your marketing plan must include goals so that you know where to aim your marketing efforts. It must include strategies designed to help you reach your goal, and it must include marketing tactics that help to advance your marketing strategies. Many lawyers implement tactics without regard for whether or not those tactics are part of the overall plan and often find that their efforts are wasted. If you need help in designing and implementing your marketing plan, don't hesitate to get it.

The New Client

6

IF YOU MARKET YOUR PRACTICE SUCCESSFULLY, many people will call you seeking help with their personal injury claims. That is why you market your practice: to make the telephone ring. In thinking about dealing with callers, ask yourself why clients call a personal injury lawyer in the first place. Is it because they want to hire a lawyer? Is it because they want to file a lawsuit? Is it because they want to spend the next year or two fighting with an insurance company? It is probably not for any of those reasons. It is more likely because they have been hurt in an accident and don't know where to turn. They need someone to guide them through the legal system. Your Yellow Pages ad says that you help people. That's why they call you.

Your job is to let them know that you will provide them with safety and security. Your job is to let them know that you will make sure that no one takes advantage of them. "They will have to get past me to get to you" is what they want you to say. "Not over my dead body" is what they hope you will promise them. You not only have to say it, you have to mean it too.

Only a few people out of the general population ever have to make a claim for injuries, much less hire a lawyer to fight their battle for them. When they find

We will help you. Call us!
Be Style & Security

71

themselves in such a situation, they have no frame of reference, no experience that they can draw on to tell them what to expect. They are sailing in uncharted waters. When they call you or come into your office, all they really want to know is whether you will help them. In advising them at that first meeting, your job is simply to do the following:

1. Answer their questions.
2. Tell them whether you can help them.
3. Do what you say you will do.

If you know at the first meeting that you cannot help the client or don't want to take the case, tell the person so. Clients will be less disappointed if you are direct with them than if you get their hopes up and then later decline to take the case.

Taking Their Calls

Many clients report that when they call a law office for the first time, they cannot get through to the lawyer. "She will call you back" is what they are told, but "She's not interested in you" is what they hear. Why spend time and money to get people to call you if you don't care enough to talk with them when they call?

So what is the best way to handle that first call? Start by having staff members who can speak with the caller about his or her problem in a helpful and professional manner. Provide training for all your staff members on telephone procedures, including courteous treatment of callers. Videotapes and pamphlets are available through the ABA as well as other bar organizations.

Some calls will be for types of cases that you do not handle. If you have established a referral relationship with one or more other lawyers for non-PI cases, your staff person should be able to refer the caller to the other lawyer directly, without your having to speak to the caller. In some cases it will be clear to your staff person that the caller has a problem that is completely out of your area of practice and will refer the caller to a lawyer referral service. One situation in which you should speak with the client directly is if he or she has a case that you don't handle, but you are trying to develop a referral relationship with a lawyer who does handle such cases. You should speak with the caller, and then (with the caller's permission) call the lawyer directly to find out if the lawyer is interested in taking the case. You can then help arrange a meeting or phone conversation between the caller and the lawyer.

If the caller has a personal injury claim, a lawyer or legal assistant should speak with the caller immediately. Taking a moment to speak directly with a prospective client can generate enormous good will. It may be that the prospective client has a very good case and is calling around for a lawyer who is available to speak with him or her right away. You may miss a golden opportunity.

Legal assistants are key members of the legal team, and clients will normally be happy to have a legal assistant take the time to listen to their story and schedule a personal meeting or telephone conference with the lawyer. The legal assistants should mail intake information to the client the same day she calls. Regardless of who speaks with the prospective client, there is key information that should be written down. A sample of an initial contact report collecting such information is provided in Appendix D.

Meeting in Person

Believe it or not, many personal injury lawyers rarely meet with clients. Legal assistants or other staff members handle all client contact. These lawyers do not meet clients unless it is absolutely necessary, such as before a deposition or other court proceeding. Many of these lawyers send the client a fee agreement by mail and communicate only in writing or on the telephone. Since many cases settle before a lawsuit has been filed, these lawyers may never meet the client. This is a dangerous way to practice law.

Take the time to meet your clients before you accept their cases. Give them a chance to talk with you and to ask you questions. It is only fair that you give them that courtesy. Some PI lawyers in every community have the reputation for running a "mill," where a high volume of cases are processed with no personal service. You do not want to develop that reputation.

Furthermore, it is to your advantage to meet each of your clients and to get to know them. You will be able to provide better service and, it is hoped, to get better results for them.

Don't Use Jargon

When you meet with a client, don't talk "like a lawyer." Don't lapse into legal jargon. Tell the client in plain language what you are going to do for him or her. A bright, young lawyer was heard to answer a client's question about the settlement of her case by telling her this:

> We will need to tender the offer to the underinsurance carrier because they have a subrogation interest against the adverse insured. Then they will have thirty days to accept or reject the tender. If they reject the tender, then they will have to step into the shoes of the adverse carrier with respect to policy limits. . . .

Judging from the incredulous look on the client's face, the better answer may have been this one: "We will need about a month to work out the details with the two insurance companies, but after that you should get your money."

What the young lawyer said was perfectly accurate, but it made no sense at all to the client and, what is worse, did not make her feel any better. The second answer would have been equally accurate and have made the client feel a lot better as well. Remember that clients want you to help them and to care about what happens to them. Make sure that you convey that sense of caring in the way that you speak to the client. Care enough to use words and phrases that the client understands.

Speaking of being understood, if you are speaking with a client whose preferred language is not English, care enough to arrange for an interpreter who can make sure that everything you say is completely understood. Usually the client can bring in a friend or relative to interpret. If it is hard to understand lawyers when they are speaking English, imagine what they must sound like if a client's native language is Spanish or Russian.

Getting All the Facts

How can you know whether you can take care of a new client without knowing everything about the client's case? Most of the time, lawyers do not learn the important facts until long after they have committed to take the client's case. It is natural for clients to put their best foot forward when meeting with a personal injury lawyer. You should expect that when they tell you about the accident or their stay at the hospital or their injury from that defective product, they will want to give you mostly "good news"—that is, news that will make their case sound good and will make you want to help them. However, in your quest to get all the facts, you will want to ask them a few questions to find out who actually ran the red light and caused the accident. You will want to find out about those other accidents in which the client suffered the same back injury.

In addition, if you are the second or third lawyer that the client has consulted about this case, you will want to find out what facts caused the other lawyers to turn it down. Not that you should turn down a case just because other lawyers didn't take it, but you should be curious about why they turned it down. With each successive lawyer the client will naturally improve the "sales pitch" to avoid another turndown. That may involve leaving out some of the negatives that turned off the first few lawyers. It is up to you to get the whole story from clients without seeming like you are "grilling" them.

One approach taken by a colleague of mine is to agree to take the client's case, with the understanding that the lawyer will investigate the claim, get all of the client's medical records, and meet with the client's doctor before filing suit or taking any action on the case. No reasonable client could object to that arrangement.

Be sure to use a new client intake form. A sample form for use in the initial interview is provided in Appendix E. This form forces you to take the time to get all the information you need about the case. If your practice has been to get the client's name and address on a yellow pad with a few cryptic notes about the accident, the intake form will take some getting used to for you. However, if it seems too hard to do, keep in mind that it is far easier to turn down new clients during that first meeting than after you have accepted the case. So get everything you need to help you decide. Be sure to get the information about the adverse party and check for any conflicts. Your check may be a manual check of your old client lists or, ideally, you can query the computer to see if any names come up.

As stated earlier, not all lawyers participate in the first meeting with a prospective client. Some delegate the job to a legal assistant or other staff member if they are unavailable. Depending on your volume of cases and your court schedule, you may not have the time to personally interview every prospective client. Still, in a personal injury case more than in any other type of case, your evaluation of the client's credibility, believability, demeanor, and other subjective factors needs to be factored in to the decision to take the case or to turn it down. An experienced legal assistant will be able to evaluate those characteristics and will probably be right as often as a lawyer.

Nonetheless, since you are the lawyer who will have to present that client to the jury if the case doesn't settle, you would be wise to spend at least a few minutes with every prospective client at the first meeting to make sure that the chemistry is right and that you share the legal assistant's impression of the client.

Auditioning

In most cases the client will be ready to hire you after the first visit with you or your legal assistant. In some cases, however, the prospective client will be "auditioning" lawyers before deciding which lawyer to hire. The client will sometimes tell you this during the first telephone call. Other times you won't hear about it until the end of the first interview, when the client says that she or he has some other lawyers to meet with but will be making a decision soon.

These auditions are not generally liked by lawyers. The interview often includes such questions as "How good are you?" or "What is your record?" Some prospective clients will even ask for references. The truth is that most lawyers don't keep track of their "win-loss record," and the client is usually satisfied if you simply describe the extent of your experience in handling similar cases. If the case is one that is likely to go to trial rather than settling, you can tell the client about your trial experience, thereby providing reassurance that the client will be well served in the courtroom.

Lawyers are usually more tolerant of such auditions if the case is novel or complex (or really big) than if the case is fairly ordinary or routine (or really small). Some lawyers routinely include their legal assistant or associate in the first meeting with a new client, especially in a big case. They will often arrange for a nurse or other medically trained person to meet with the client as well. The client will be pleased and impressed with your efforts, and you will be better able to evaluate the case after speaking with the others who attended the meeting with you.

Signing Fee Agreements

Most states require a signed contingency fee agreement, and many states will specify what needs to be included in the agreement. Some states provide a statutory cancellation period in which the client can get out of a fee agreement without owing the lawyer anything. Regardless of whether such a fee agreement is required in your state or jurisdiction, you should make sure that every new client signs one. The agreement should specify how you are to be paid; whether the percentage goes up at the time of trial or arbitration; whether it will be you or the client who pays the costs of the case; how you will be repaid for any costs that you advance; and how you will be paid in the event that the client decides to change lawyers during the case.

Send the new client a copy of the signed agreement, along with a letter explaining what the client can do to help collect medical records and the like and thanking the client for retaining you in the case. A sample of this initial letter to the client is included among the letters in Appendix J.

The Confidential Client Questionnaire

The initial interview form will give you only cursory information about your new client. A confidential client questionnaire will supplement that form and tell you virtually everything about your new client. Appendix F contains a sample of a client questionnaire.

Often clients will not know what information about their history is important and relevant to the case and what is not. In personal injury cases especially, what is relevant in one case may not matter in another. The confidential client questionnaire should ask for information about the following:

- Previous names and addresses
- Employment history
- Education
- Marital and family information (including prior marriages and significant relationships)
- Complete medical history
- Prior injuries
- Arrests and convictions
- Accident history, including motor vehicle accidents and on-the-job injuries
- Workers' compensation claims history
- Other insurance claims
- Previous lawyers

New clients should be made to understand that once they make a claim for injuries, their lives become an open book. Most people do not welcome this invasion of their privacy, but you can reassure clients that you will be in a better position to protect their privacy if you have all the information in advance instead of first hearing about it during a deposition or, worst of all, at trial.

Many people cannot recall their last three addresses and the dates that they lived there or all the jobs that they have held during the past ten years. It will be easier for everyone if you give clients the questionnaire with instructions to take it home and fill it out. Be sure to give them a deadline and send a follow-up letter if the questionnaire has not been returned by that date. If they still do not respond, schedule an appointment with them to go over the completed form. Make it clear that you cannot proceed with their case unless and until you get the questionnaire back. If they seem reluctant to complete the form, it may be because there is information about their past that they do not want to disclose, even to their lawyer. Without the questionnaire, they can avoid disclosing embarrassing information by claiming (rightly or wrongly) that you never asked them about it.

Another benefit of the questionnaire is that it allows you to gauge the degree of cooperation that you can expect from your client. As every lawyer who has tried a case knows, the client who is actively involved in the case and cooperates with you in developing the case has a better chance of getting a good result than the client who is uninvolved and passive. Many people are willing to "give their case" to a lawyer, thinking that they won't have to do anything more. They should understand that the time they will spend filling out the questionnaire will be far less than they will have to spend preparing for and attending depositions, undergoing medical examinations by insurance company doctors, and preparing for and attending the trial.

After you have succeeded in getting the completed questionnaire back from the client, be sure to schedule a face-to-face meeting so that you can go over the questionnaire together. Since you asked the client to take the time to get you the information, you should show the client that the information is important and necessary to the case by sitting down with him or her and discussing it. Such a meeting gives the client an opportunity to explain any potentially embarrassing entries as well. It also helps you to get to know the client.

Selecting Cases

You won't be able to, and won't want to, take every case that will be presented to you. If you are fortunate, you will get many calls from people with good cases. Others will be from people with bad cases. Yet others will be from people with potentially good cases. The problem for you lies in telling the difference between these types of cases.

A bad case is one where no amount of hard work on your part will make a difference. No amount of time spent by you can make that traffic light turn out to be green for your client. You can't build a practice on bad cases, so you will need to learn how to recognize them right away. What makes a case bad? It may be bad for a number of reasons. For example, liability may be weak; you may not be able to prove the connection between the accident and the claimed injuries; or the client may have had other injuries unrelated to the accident that are more likely the cause of his or her present medical problems.

You might think that bad cases are easy to spot, but they aren't. If you take a bad case occasionally, don't feel alone. It happens to everyone. Young lawyers especially are likely to take a bad case, thinking that it will turn into a good case. Just remember that a good case occasionally may turn bad, but a bad case rarely turns good. You have to learn to say no to people. Just because they think that they have a good case doesn't mean that you have to agree with them. Practice saying "No." Practice with your staff in a mock interview. Find a way to decline a case that will allow you and the prospective client to part company in a professional manner. In addition, after your meeting always send a turndown letter advising the client of the statute of limitations. A letter explaining that you are turning down a case is included among the sample letters in Appendix J.

Be Selective

There will be both good and bad aspects to a potentially good case, and it is hard to say at first which side will prevail. You can tell that a lot of hard work and money might make the difference between a good result and a bad one, but often you can't judge how much of either it will take. In your optimism and desire to please the client, it will be easy to underestimate what it will take to win.

You should limit the number of these cases that you take at any one time because they demand so much of your time and money. If you are working a large number of risky cases and none of them comes through, you could be put in a difficult financial situation. If you take a case and it later turns bad, don't be afraid to admit that it hasn't lived up to your hopes. Make sure that the client is someone who will listen to your advice and either settle or drop the case if your investigation doesn't bear fruit. Even if the case turns out to be one that you cannot win, the client might be grateful for your hard work and recommend you to friends and family.

Discussing the Client's Objectives

Isn't the objective of every personal injury case to get the other side to pay you what the claim is worth? Isn't the objective to get fair value or else take the case to trial? Not necessarily. Not if your client makes it clear that she is not willing to subject herself to a long and grueling jury trial. Not if your client has an unsavory past that would turn a jury against him. Not if your client is in such a precarious financial position that he cannot afford to gamble that he can improve on the pretrial offer. In such cases, you need to establish a different objective.

Money is the usual objective in personal injury cases. The clients want compensation for their injuries. Sometimes clients may want a "day in court" to vent their anger or frustration, but that is not common. In fact, most clients do not want to go to court. One defense lawyer remarked that the plaintiff's fear of going to trial is one of the major factors working in favor of the defense.

When they first come to see you, however, clients often have no objective other than to be treated fairly by the insurance company that has made a low-ball offer or refused to fix the car or refused to pay for medical bills or lost wages. The best way to begin the discussion of objectives with your client is simply to ask what the client's objectives are, and then listen carefully. You may be surprised at what you learn. Not all clients have the same objectives, and any client's objectives may change during the case.

Objective 1: Settling Early

Often the client is not interested in holding out for top dollar. Try asking your client how much he or she would like to net from a settlement. It may be that the client's range is closer than you think to what the other side is prepared to pay. In such cases, you need to be cautious about telling clients that their expectations are too low. Many lawyers have talked clients out of settling, only to have the jury come back with a low verdict or, worse yet, a defense verdict. It is good counseling for the lawyer to encourage the client to reject an unreasonably low offer in a good case. However, to encourage the client to reject a reasonable offer and take unreasonable risks is bad counseling and worse lawyering.

Objective 2: Settling the Case for Any Amount

This objective is appropriate in cases where the client needs money desperately or has skeletons in the closet that would be discovered and ruin the case later on if the case were litigated. You may not even want to take such a case, but if you do, be sure to outline the situation in writing and get the client's agreement to seek an early settlement. If the client's financial situation has led her or him to settle for less than the case is worth, advise the client in writing of your opinion as to the value of the case if it were to go to trial or arbitration. If the early settlement is because of the client's past, explain how prior injuries, insurance claims, or criminal conduct may be admissible in court if the case were to go that far.

Objective 3: Settling for as Much Money as Possible Without Going to Trial

It is difficult to get top dollar from a case if the other side knows or suspects that your client has cold feet and is unwilling to go to trial. Sometimes it is effective to lead the other side to believe that your client is willing to go "all the way" if necessary. Many clients who do not want to go to trial are willing to do what is necessary short of going to trial. That may involve turning down an early "low-ball" offer, filing a lawsuit, going through depositions, and actually getting the case ready for trial. This strategy is particularly good when you have a solid case and the other side, for one reason or another, has simply failed to appreciate how solid your case really is. What you are counting on is that the other side will see the folly of their position after you give them a chance to see your evidence during the discovery process. The key to this strategy is that your case has to be as solid as you think it is. If you are correct, you may get better offers as the trial draws closer. However, if you are incorrect and get surprised with bad evidence during discovery, you may find yourself close to trial with no settlement offer on the horizon. Moreover, in some cases the other side may withdraw an offer that was previously extended to you.

Many insurance companies have adopted a policy of giving their best offer early in the case and not increasing it. The problem for plaintiffs' lawyers is that they never know for sure if they have gotten the final and best offer from the other side. As you gain experience and get to know the lawyers and claims representatives in your city, you will get to know their negotiating styles.

Mediation and other alternative dispute resolution (ADR) techniques are often helpful in accomplishing the objective of getting top dollar for your client's case. Neither side wants to go through a mediation session without settling the case, so it is often possible for a mediator to get the other side to pay more than it originally intended to pay to settle the case.

Objective 4: Holding Out for Top Dollar— Going All the Way

Often the client tells you early in the case that he or she expects to be fully compensated for injuries and is not willing to settle for an amount that the client believes would be even slightly on the low side. The first issue for the lawyer is to decide whether the client's optimism is warranted. If you disagree with the client's assessment of the value of the case and the likelihood of winning at trial, you will need to discuss that with the client. You may want to try to persuade the client to see the case differently. On the other hand, if you and the client agree that the case is a good one, that the offer is inadequate, and that there is no likelihood that the other side will increase its offer substantially, your objective will probably be to try the case to a jury (or to an arbitrator in some jurisdictions) in hopes of getting what you think the case is worth. Even if this becomes your objective, you must remain flexible in case the other side increases its offer or in case your evidence turns bad.

Colleagues of mine debate whether you should file suit early in the case or only as a last resort after negotiations have failed. Some view the filing of a lawsuit as an unnecessary extra expense and point out that as soon as a complaint is filed, you are bound by court deadlines and lose some flexibility in managing the case. What's worse, they point out, once you file, the defense lawyers will bombard you with discovery requests. Other colleagues claim that only after they file suit do the insurance companies begin to take their claims seriously. Some of those lawyers routinely "file everything" and claim that they always get more by way of settlement or trial than if they had never filed the case.

If your plan is to file suit and "go all the way" to trial, you should begin early to prepare your client for the trial. Rehearsing trial testimony, working with a trial consultant in some cases, and preparing for the stress of a trial—whether it is planned to last for a day, a week, or a month—should commence early in the process. Be sure to advise the client to arrange for time off from work and to make child-care plans and other arrangements so that there are no conflicts or distractions during the time of the trial.

Keeping Personal Injury Clients Happy | **7**

$\mathbf{T}$HE REALITY OF CLIENT RELATIONS is that even when you are trying your hardest, you won't be able to keep all your clients happy all the time. However, if you don't try hard all the time, everyone will be unhappy. When clients are unhappy, they either call and complain or fire you and get another lawyer. Lawyers don't like it when their clients call to complain, but it's better than having them call another lawyer.

Why Clients Become Unhappy

Most people have no idea of what is in store for them when they file a claim or a lawsuit for personal injuries. They have never had to deal with the endless delays and postponements that are part of any lawsuit. They have never had to undergo medical examinations by insurance company-paid doctors. They have never had their lives become subject to intense scrutiny by claims adjusters. They have never had depositions taken by skeptical and unrelenting defense lawyers.

Personal injury clients may become unhappy more easily than other people because of the very fact that they have been injured. They may be off work and losing income; they may be facing surgery; or they may have already had surgery and found it hasn't helped. They may become unhappy because no one takes their injuries seriously. Often their injuries result in serious financial difficulties, which in turn put a strain on their personal relationships. If, on top of all that, they have chronic pain that they must deal with every day, they may occasionally lose patience with the process and explode at you, their lawyer. Why do they explode at you? Because you told them in the beginning that you would make everything work out fine and you promised to run interference for them. Now they find that the wolves are at the door and you aren't helping much. They may conclude that you're no longer on their side. In fact, many times when people call another lawyer because they're thinking of firing their current lawyer, they will complain that their lawyer doesn't seem to be fighting for them. Those perceptions may or may not be legitimate, but you need to deal with their concerns or you will lose those clients.

Clients become unhappy because their lawyer doesn't take their phone calls or return their calls. How do *you* feel when you phone someone in a business setting and that person won't take your call? Do you interpret that conduct to be a sign of support? Of course not. It is a sign of indifference, at best. You would not want to do business with that person. Your clients feel the same way when you do it to them.

Clients also become unhappy when their lawyer won't meet with them in person to discuss the case. When they call to make an appointment, they are told that they don't "need" an appointment or that the lawyer is too busy. They interpret this to mean "your case isn't important enough for me to be bothered." How would you like to be represented by some professional who refuses to meet with you? Take time to meet with your clients and tell them what is going on now and what will happen in the future. Give them some timelines to work with so they won't be expecting something to happen this week when, in fact, nothing will happen for three months.

Many times lawyers put themselves in a bad situation by promising the client a lot in the beginning simply to "sign up" the client. Once the fee agreement has been signed, the honeymoon is over and the new client becomes just another client. The poor client, however, has no way of knowing that his or her status will decrease so soon. The client may wonder why the lawyer, who was so personable and charming in the beginning, now won't even talk to her or him. Can you blame the client for becoming angry and frustrated?

Another way that lawyers set themselves up for problems is by making unrealistic promises just to sign up the client. Later, when the lawyer is ready to settle the case for an amount that is less than the lawyer originally predicted, the client will be surprised and disappointed.

How to Keep Clients Happy

You can keep clients happy by following these five rules:

1. Don't make promises that you can't keep.
2. Don't treat your clients any differently than you would want to be treated.
3. Work hard for your clients.
4. Tell your clients how hard you are working for them.
5. Communicate with them regularly.

Don't Make Promises That You Can't Keep

Making unrealistic promises may help you get the client in the beginning, but it will lead to disaster later. People appreciate sincerity and honesty, and if you demonstrate those qualities in the beginning, you are just as likely to get the client as if you exaggerate. Draw on your experience to tell new clients what they can expect if they make a claim or file a lawsuit. If a client comes to you with unrealistic expectations, you will be doing the client and yourself a disservice by encouraging them. Why would you want to take on a client who has expectations to which you will never be able to live up? Sooner or later you would have to disappoint that client, and disappointed clients often file bar complaints against their lawyers.

Don't Treat Clients Any Differently Than You Would Want to Be Treated

This really shouldn't have to be said, but the best way to keep your clients happy is to treat them with the courtesy and respect that you would demand if you were the client.

Work Hard for Your Clients

Only you can say whether you are working hard for your client. Working hard means that you know at all times what is going on with your client's case and you have a plan to accomplish the remaining tasks. It also means that you give the case regular attention and direct your staff to show the same concern for the case. Many lawyers sign up the client, then give the file to a legal assistant and expect the legal assistant to make everything happen without further involvement by the lawyer. Those lawyers become detached from their cases and, as a result, detached from their clients. There is always something that can be done on a case— even if it is to reread the documents in the file. Those who say "work smarter, not harder" overlook the fact that sometimes hard work—real drudgery—is needed to move a case along successfully. Maybe working harder is the smart thing to do.

Tell Your Clients How Hard You Are Working for Them

Clients often have no idea what is going on with their case, and if you don't tell them they will never find out. Worse yet, they assume that nothing is going on because they never hear from you. An effective way to let clients know what you are doing for them is to e-mail or call them and tell them. Tell them what has happened since you last spoke together. Tell them what you are doing now and what you plan to do in the future. Give them a long-term assessment of the case. Ask them if they have any questions or concerns and offer to meet with them in person if they want. While you are taking the time to talk with them, get an update on their medical or employment situation so that you can document the file for future reference. The client will appreciate your efforts and you will generate some important good will.

Communicate with Clients Regularly

Regularity is the key to effective communication with clients. Send your clients copies of all correspondence that you send to others as well as copies of all correspondence that you receive concerning their case. Encourage clients to call if there is anything that they don't understand in any of the documents. Ask the client to call you every two weeks to check in.

Ask Your Clients How You Are Doing

If you regularly keep in touch with your clients and keep them informed, you will have many more happy clients than unhappy clients. Your clients will not fire you in the middle of a case because you won't return their phone calls.

To measure how you are doing overall, provide your clients with a client service questionnaire to complete and return anonymously at the conclusion of the case. A client service questionnaire is provided in Appendix G.

Working with Employees, Contractors, and Other Professionals

8

ONCE YOU HAVE SUCCEEDED in attracting new clients, your focus will shift from getting work to getting the work out. To manage your workload successfully, you will need good staff and good systems.

Working with Staff

Selecting and keeping good staff is essential to success in a personal injury practice. No matter how good a lawyer you are, you can be no better than the people around you. If you hire hardworking, motivated people and treat them well, they will stay with you and help you build your practice.

Your staff requirements will vary depending on your type of practice, whether you are specialized, your volume of cases, and a host of other factors. Both the number of personnel that you will need and the skills that they will have to possess will depend on these factors. If you are just starting out in private practice with a small caseload, you may have one part-time or shared employee or no staff at all. As you build your practice and begin to add staff as necessary, you will need to determine what tasks you want to delegate to your staff. If you do have staff, including as few as one part-time assistant or secretary, here are some questions that will help you evaluate your staff's effectiveness.

How Does Your Staff Handle the Quantity of Work?

Is your staff/assistant able to accomplish their work in a timely manner? Are all deadlines being met? Is work being finished "just in time" or well in advance of deadlines? If your staff/assistant is chronically behind in getting the work done or is getting it done at the last minute, is it because they aren't working hard enough or because there is too much work for them to handle? Alternatively, is it because you failed to implement systems and procedures that would bring some order to the office?

If yours is a high-volume personal injury practice, but your staffing is geared toward a low-volume, specialty practice, your staff/assistant will have trouble keeping up with the workload no matter how hard they try. Most personal injury lawyers handle a mix of cases—some auto accident cases, some slip-and-fall cases, and a few medical malpractice and products liability cases. The greater the mix of cases, the more important it will be to have a staff/assistant that can respond to the challenge.

Does the Quality of Your Staff/Assistant's Work Meet Your Standards?

Judging quality is largely a subjective process, but there are ways that you can measure quality in your personal injury practice. Take a moment to look at the work product that you and the members of your staff produce. Are you always pleased with the quality of the documents that your staff/assistant produces? Is the staff/assistant courteous to clients and other callers and visitors? Do you ever get surprised during a deposition or hearing with facts of which you should have been aware? Does your staff/assistant ever fail to subpoena an important witness? If you are experiencing problems with quality, is it because of lack of effort, lack of ability, lack of training, or some other reason? Is it because there is no personal accountability for work product?

Before you judge the quality of your staff/assistant's work, consider what your employees see when they look at your work. What kind of example are you setting? Do you always practice professionalism and high ethical standards? Do you insist on being thoroughly prepared for every deposition, hearing, or court appearance? Do you spend enough time at the office? Do you return your clients' phone calls punctually? Are you willing to sacrifice your time to get a job done right? Do you have a reputation for diligence and honesty among other members of the bar? Remember that wherever you lead, your staff will follow. If you set an example of professionalism, your staff will be professional too.

Do You Have the Right Mix of Staff?

If you have more than one employee (or contractor), you should have a job description for each position. Do your legal team members have the right complement of skills, knowledge, and experience to allow them to work together effectively? Do you have the right balance of clerical, secretarial, paralegal, and legal staff? Do you have staff with medical records training or nursing or paramedic experience?

Many personal injury firms look for legal assistants who have experience as insurance claims adjusters. With that kind of experience, assistants can be effective in preparing cases for settlement and in giving you insights into how particular insurance companies and law firms evaluate and handle cases. Legal assistants can also take part, under your supervision, in negotiating case settlements directly with insurance company representatives. The extent of a legal assistant's role is, of course, subject to ethics considerations, and legal assistants should not be asked to take on responsibilities that are beyond their training or abilities.

The more your staff can work independently and exercise professional judgment, the less you will have to be involved in making day-to-day decisions. If you strive to make certain that each task is performed by the individual whose skills are most appropriate to the task, you and your staff will be far more productive (and happy).

Are You Doing the Right Work?

The first question is: How do you spend your day? Look at what you do all day and determine whether it fits your skills and qualifications. Are you doing work that could be better done by someone else? Is someone else doing your work? If you are doing the wrong work, find out why and make some changes. It may be that in doing the wrong work, you are creating a bottleneck and preventing your staff from getting work done in a timely and orderly fashion.

Many lawyers, including PI lawyers, lack the experience or temperament to delegate work effectively, and they attempt to micromanage every task in the office. They haven't learned that the best results are achieved by hiring qualified people, and then delegating appropriate tasks to them and stepping back and letting them do their work. Many trial lawyers complain that they have to be at the office night and day to get their work done, when their real problem is that they don't know how to use their time effectively.

Hiring Good Employees

A personal injury law office requires an extraordinary amount of teamwork in preparing cases for trial. When a big case finally gets to trial, the entire staff must be ready. Whether your trial will last for several days or several months, your staff needs to pull together. You will need people who can work as a team, who can put differences aside for the good of the team, and who can assume any role necessary to help the team accomplish its goal. It may mean working long hours and facing unreasonable demands. It may also mean being creative in figuring out how to get other work done at the same time. Your staff people will have to contend with adjournments, postponements, and court holidays. They will have to be creative in dealing with the crises that invariably occur while you are in the courtroom, unavailable to provide assistance. They will need to be decisive.

There are two options for hiring employees for the personal injury practice: (1) hire people without experience and train them, and (2) hire seasoned veterans. The more specialized the position is, the less likely it will be that you can provide the needed training. You can't train someone to be a nurse or a claims adjuster, but you can train someone to be a paralegal or a secretary.

Prospective employees can be located through public and private placement services; through local, state, and national professional organizations; and through informal sources such as other lawyers or legal staff. In addition, you may personally know someone desirous of joining your staff.

Hiring Friends and Family

There are advantages and disadvantages to hiring friends and family. Among the advantages, a friend or relative who has no legal experience may be willing to be trained for the job and to work for a low salary in the beginning while you are building your practice. Friends and relatives are often more loyal and protective of your interests and will stay with you longer than a stranger would. Because of your relationship, they may not be as tempted to leave for another job, even if it means more money. Nonetheless, when you bring family into the office, you risk bringing a new set of problems to the practice. People who have a healthy personal relationship and communicate well have a better chance of making a work relationship work. Likewise, however, if there are strains in the personal relationship, there will probably be strains in the work relationship.

Using Staff Effectively

Establishing policies and procedures will help standardize the way that cases are handled and ensure consistency in case management. Disorganization is a problem for any law firm, but it is especially a problem for a personal injury firm with a lot of clients. At any time, you will have any number of clients who are still under treatment by their doctor, others who have concluded treatment and are ready to settle, and others who are in various stages of litigation. In addition to keeping track of what needs to be done on every case, your staff must be able to respond to inquiries from you, from the clients, and from an assortment of other people involved in the cases. In such an environment, it is easy for things to be missed. A good system and set of procedures will minimize the chances for errors to occur.

Assigning Work

If you are the only lawyer and you have only one staff person, assigning work is not a problem. However, if you have more than one staff member or there is more than one lawyer, you need to allocate the work among the staff. When one lawyer has more than one staff member, there are two methods for assigning work:

- ◆ Method 1: Each staff member is fully responsible for a case from start to finish.
- ◆ Method 2: Staff members work together on cases, but each has responsibility for certain tasks. (For example, one person would be responsible for obtaining medical records for all cases.)

Each method has advantages and disadvantages. With the first method, the advantage is that the staff member responsible for handling a case will know that case inside and out. The disadvantage is that the person may be performing tasks that are above or below his or her level of expertise. Every case involves a wide variety of tasks, from routine clerical tasks to analysis of medical records and other documents, to legal research and trial preparation. A legal assistant with a lot of experience and a high level of skill will be underutilized if he or she has to perform lower-level tasks. It is more efficient and cost-effective to assign the lower-level tasks to someone who does not have the skills of the experienced legal assistant. By assigning work in this manner, you will better utilize both employees and should save in salary costs as well. A sample form for assigning tasks ranging from human resources management to trials and ADR is provided in Appendix H.

Instilling a Sense of Urgency

In personal injury litigation, the lawyers on the other side normally get paid by the hour. They are never in a hurry to conclude a case. They send out their standard requests for production, interrogatories, and subpoenas, and then analyze every document for any inconsistencies. That takes time—a lot of time. You, on the other hand, don't get paid until the case settles. You need to do whatever you can to move the case along toward its conclusion. If early in the case you provide the other side with every possible document and take the initiative in scheduling depositions, it may help get the case settled and it may help get the case to trial more quickly than if a lot of loose ends remained untied.

You must instill in your staff a sense of urgency so that they will not put off tasks until tomorrow. There are few firm deadlines in a plaintiff's practice. Lawsuits don't have to be filed at any particular point in time (except for statutes of limitations); depositions can always be put off another week or two; and trial dates always seem to get postponed once or twice before the case actually gets to court. In short, a plaintiff's practice is a procrastinator's dream—you can put off everything indefinitely and no one cares. You should care.

Whoever is responsible for working with you on a particular case should have to tell you how long it has been since the client was medically stationary and why the case isn't ready for settlement. They should have to tell you how long it has been since the lawsuit was filed and why the case hasn't been considered for an ADR program such as mediation or arbitration. Your staff needs to see you as a person who demands action and who won't tolerate procrastination. You should also consider a compensation program that encourages prompt action. Such a program would involve setting target dates for getting particular cases resolved and rewarding your employees for beating those target dates.

Establishing Systems and Procedures

You need information to be an effective lawyer, and you need information to be an effective manager. Set up a system, preferably a computerized one, that can provide you with the following reports instantly:

1. Master Client List
2. Cases by Date Opened

3. Cases by Statute of Limitations
4. Cases by Injury Type
5. Cases by Lawyer/Legal Assistant
6. Filed/Unfiled Cases
7. Cases by Trial/Arbitration/Mediation Dates
8. Cases Ready for Settlement

By having these reports available to you and your staff, you will be able to stay current on the status of every case and to make inquiries when a case doesn't appear on a particular report. It is much easier for a case to languish in a file drawer or on someone's desk when you never ask about it. After you inquire about it once or twice, your staff will get the message that you are interested in seeing some action on that case.

Software programs are available for every aspect of a personal injury practice. Start by investing in a case management program that comes in a network version so that everyone in your office can have access to the same information. Even if you are starting out with only a secretary and yourself, you still need a computerized system. (Computer software considerations are discussed in Chapter 10.) There are many software packages available for the small law office that will automate most case-related activities, such as reports, docket control, conflict checking, and form letters. Invest in training so you and your staff can learn the new system, and commit to using it yourself. If you don't use systems, your staff won't either. Software information is available through the ABA Legal Technology Resource Center, and programs are advertised and reviewed in such publications as *Law Practice* magazine, published by the ABA Law Practice Management Section, and *Trial*, published by ATLA.

Also, buy a good calendar system for your computer network so that you and your staff can coordinate scheduling of appointments, trials, vacations, and other activities. The calendar program must have the ability to create to-do lists and "tickler" or follow-up dates. Use the calendar faithfully. Don't make your staff have to chase you down and ask you to check your pocket calendar for an available deposition date. (Many lawyers still do this.) Set your calendar system to remind you every thirty days to review every file, even if there are no tickler dates during that period. No file should go longer than that without having someone review it to see what needs to be done to move the case along.

Most word processing programs allow the PI lawyer to generate fill-in-the-blank forms for correspondence and pleadings. Preset macros (routines built into word processing programs) let the user perform automated tasks such as inserting relevant information into a letter, inserting a signature at the end of a letter or pleading, and printing an envelope.

This automation is not limited to word processing programs. Most case management programs make document creation even easier by retrieving information such as names, addresses, claims numbers, and the like from the client database and merging it into a preset form letter or other document. All you have to do is point and click with your mouse and the completed document pops out of the printer. Who needs a secretary to do that?

As part of your case evaluation process, set aside time to sit down when the phones aren't ringing and talk with your staff about the status of your cases. Find out how well the workload is balanced. Find out if there are any bottlenecks in the system and look for ways to break through them. Many times your staff will not tell you what is really going on in the office, preferring to try to handle problems themselves. If it is you who is creating the bottleneck, your staff will be hesitant to tell you. You need to ask a lot of questions. If people aren't getting tired of your questions, then you probably aren't asking enough. Your staff should view you as a fully engaged member of the team, whose objective is to do whatever is necessary to get the work out as efficiently and productively as possible.

Get a Good Bookkeeper

Even if it is only a part-time or contract bookkeeper, get someone to keep the books for you. Legal malpractice insurance companies will tell you that lawyers are much better at keeping other people's books than they are at keeping their own. If you have to choose between spending time preparing for a hearing or paying bills, your credit rating will suffer. A bookkeeper can pay your bills, balance your checkbook, and prepare financial reports for you. With software such as Quicken®, you can "write checks" by entering the information on screen and printing the checks directly to your laser printer. Quicken® will keep a running balance for your checkbook and keep track of all income and expenses by category. Your legal malpractice insurance company or professional liability fund will probably send out a practice advisor at no charge to help you set up your bookkeeping system.

Another advantage of having someone else handle the books for you is that it will force you to recognize and deal with financial emergencies. A personal injury practice is going to undergo times when the cash flow is slow. Unfortunately, during those hard times your bills still have to be paid and client costs still have to be advanced. A bookkeeper can point out upcoming financial obligations and help you avoid financial emergencies.

Many lawyers get into trouble because of the way that they handle their clients' trust accounts. A qualified bookkeeper can keep you out of that kind of trouble. Before you set up your client trust accounts, get a copy of *The ABA Guide to Lawyer Trust Accounts,* by Jay G. Foonberg (American Bar Association, Law Practice Management Section, 1996).

How to Handle Overflow

There will be times when your workload increases beyond your ability to handle it. At such times, you may be tempted to add permanent staff. Instead, you should consider bringing in temporary staff to help get you through the immediate crisis, then evaluate whether the increased workload is more than a passing phenomenon. If you are short of money for staff, there are several resources that are available in most states.

- ◆ Student Internships: Community college legal assistant programs often require students to perform an internship with a law firm. Students usually come with some recommendations by their professors. Internships may last part of a semester or longer.
- ◆ Displaced Worker Programs: Many state agencies receive money from the federal government to retrain workers

whose jobs have been eliminated because of economic dislocations. These programs provide economic incentives for employers to hire displaced workers.

◆ Injured Worker Programs: Most state vocational rehabilitation programs are eager to place workers who have left their previous jobs because of injuries but who are ready to reenter the work force. Most agencies will pay all or part of the worker's salary in exchange for job training.

When you bring in temporary workers, you must educate them about client confidentiality. Temporary workers are subject to the same ethical obligations as permanent staff and may not disclose confidential information.

Prepare for the Worst

There may come a time when an emergency strikes your office. It may come as a result of a resignation, a flood, a heart attack, or some equally devastating event. You need to prepare now for that event. In deciding whether you are prepared, consider these questions:

1. Do you have a written catastrophe plan in case of a natural emergency?
2. Do you have a written plan in case of your serious illness or death?
3. Are all policies and procedures written and organized in the event that neither you nor your staff is available to give advice?
4. Is every file thoroughly documented so that anyone could look at it and determine what has been done and what remains to be done?
5. Have you made arrangements with another lawyer or firm to provide mutual assistance in the event of an emergency?
6. Do you have an off-site backup copy of all computerized case information?
7. Do you have disability insurance that will pay for someone to come in and run your practice in the event of your illness or death?

Using Practice Advisors

Many state and local bar associations and malpractice insurance providers employ "practice advisors," professionals who are trained to assist lawyers with setting up, operating, and even closing a law practice. Most practice advisors provide their services at no charge. They will come to your office and review all your systems and procedures to help solve problems. (Practice advisors have even been known to mediate disputes between lawyers and secretaries who could not get along.) So, before hiring a consultant, consider contacting a practice management advisor, as mentioned earlier.

Personal injury lawyers routinely work with other professionals, both inside and outside of the legal profession. Lawyers often bring in more-experienced or specialized lawyers to help with a particular case. They also regularly consult with experts ranging from medical doctors to accident reconstruction engineers.

Working with Other Lawyers

Cooperation between two lawyers usually takes the form of a referral or an association of counsel. In case of a referral, one lawyer sends the case to another lawyer and the referring lawyer may not have any further contact with the case. Of course, the referring lawyer may choose to maintain some degree of involvement in the case. Some jurisdictions prohibit fee sharing when the referring lawyer does not participate in the case, and in those jurisdictions the referring lawyer has more incentive to remain actively involved so that he or she can share the fee. Referrals to PI lawyers often come from lawyers who do not practice PI law, or a referral may involve another PI lawyer who does not practice in federal court referring a case to one who does.

In the case of association of counsel, the lawyers both are counsel of record and usually participate equally in the handling of the case all the way through trial. Such arrangements often take place when the first lawyer is an experienced trial lawyer, but the second lawyer brings some special skills or experience to the case.

In complex cases involving products liability or medical malpractice, association of counsel is quite common.

Lawyers who are starting a practice and who have no trial experience may find themselves in a situation where they are facing a trial date on a case that is more complex than they had believed it to be. It then makes more sense to associate with an experienced trial lawyer, one who will let the inexperienced lawyer assist in trying the case and gain valuable experience, rather than simply referring the case and withdrawing from it. Unfortunately, many experienced lawyers do not like to co-counsel cases with inexperienced lawyers and prefer to work alone. In their zeal to get you to give them a piece of your case, they may lead you to believe that they will give you a meaningful role in the trial, only to brush you aside once you have sent them the case. A good practice is to have a referral agreement that spells out the terms of the association and gives the inexperienced lawyer the right to take the case back if the experienced lawyer will not cooperate.

Both the referral and the association of counsel should spell out who is responsible for the costs of litigation. In many cases the lawyers will share the contingency fee based on the amount of time each spends on the case and the financial risk each takes with respect to the costs. If one lawyer agrees to advance a larger share of the costs of expert witnesses, accident reconstruction, and the like, that lawyer will be able to demand a higher share of the fee if the case is successful.

Some lawyers specialize in financing undercapitalized lawyers in litigation and take a portion of the fee in return for their "venture capital." Such arrangements should be carefully reviewed for their business value as well as for their ethics.

Consulting with Other Lawyers

Sometimes beginning lawyers do not need to refer their case to or associate with another lawyer to try the case but do need some regular advice and counsel. In such cases, the lawyer can arrange to have a more experienced lawyer who will provide such advice and counsel in exchange for a fixed fee, an hourly fee, or a share of the contingency fee. This allows the inexperienced lawyer to call someone any time that problems arise and to have an experienced lawyer review pleadings, motions, and jury instructions and offer advice on strategy and tactics.

Working with Other Professionals

Personal injury lawyers deal with many cases involving medical, technical, and scientific issues, such as issues of engineering, chemistry, or hypnotherapy. In such cases, the lawyer must consult with experts in the relevant field. How and where to find such experts and how to afford their fees often are problems for newer lawyers.

A good rule of thumb is to speak openly about money before you retain the expert and to continue to speak openly about money throughout the relationship. Many new lawyers do not like to speak of money for fear that it will interfere with the relationship with the professional. Such reluctance may give the impression that money is not an issue. It is to the lawyer's advantage to let the professional know that the case is being prosecuted on a tight budget and that every consideration will be appreciated. The professional might be willing to cut the fee slightly in the face of such candor.

Expert witnesses do not work on contingency. It is unethical to do so. The new lawyer who receives an offer from an expert to testify on a contingency basis should call the local bar association and discuss his or her ethical duties to disclose such an offer and should run away from the expert witness as quickly as possible.

Managing the Workload: Case Management

9

Case management is the process of anticipating and dealing with all the activities involved in the case, from start to finish. Case management requires flexibility and adaptability because of the dynamic nature of personal injury cases. Lawyers who manage their cases well invariably get better results than lawyers who don't manage them well. Lawyers who manage their cases "by the seat of their pants" have to rely on good luck to avoid disaster. Good case management usually means the difference between success and disaster and is far more reliable than good luck.

It's not enough to forge ahead and hope for the best. Ask the lawyer who turns down a substantial pretrial settlement offer only to have the jury return a defense verdict or small award. Ask the lawyer who gets a verdict at trial only to find that it has been eaten up by the expense of getting the case to trial. Often poor management is behind these disasters. From the new client call to the final disbursement of settlement funds, a personal injury case involves a wide range of tasks, as illustrated in the accompanying flowchart.

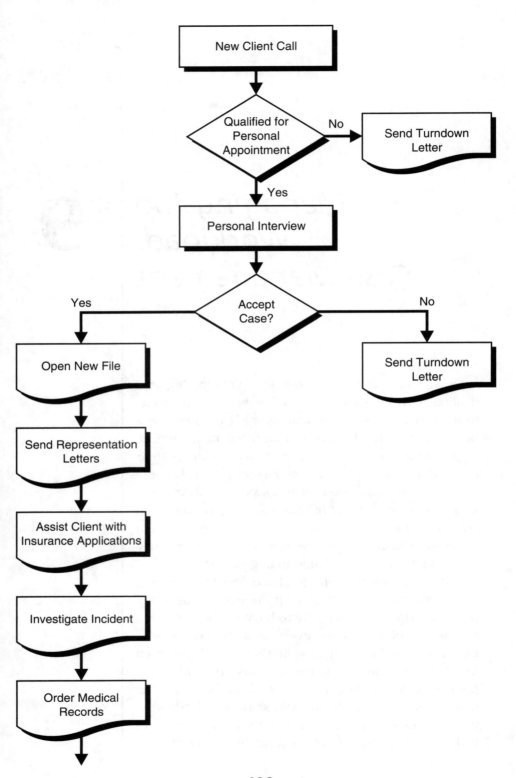

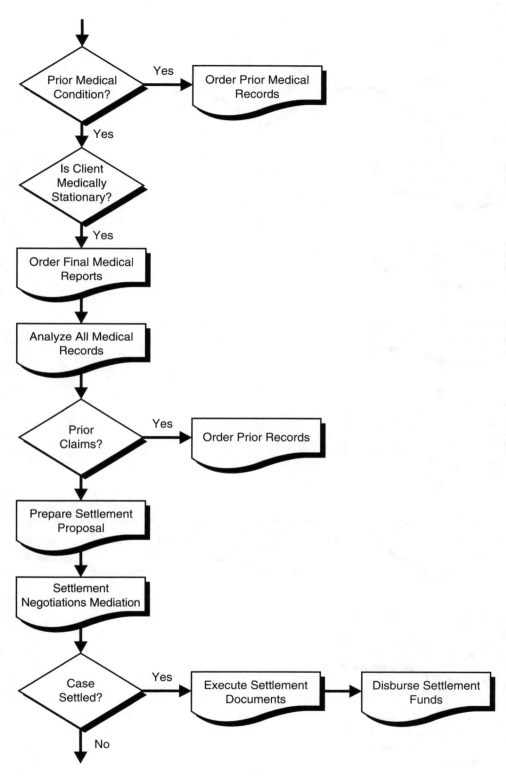

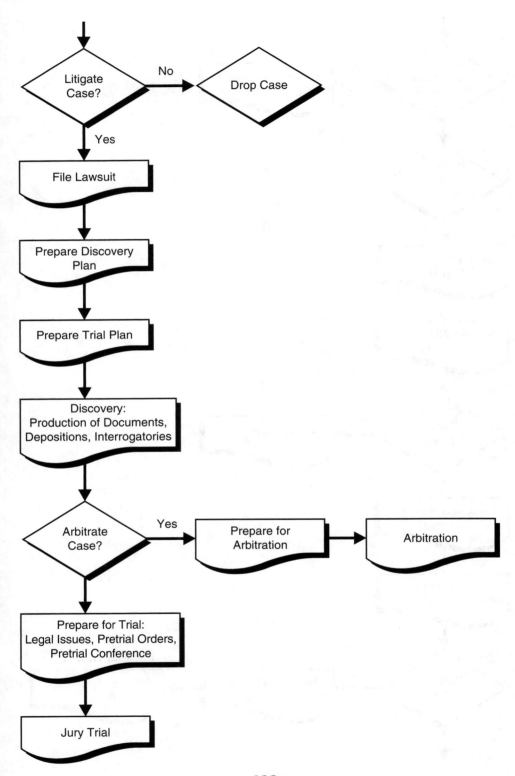

Allocating Resources

Personal injury cases require an investment of resources—that is, time and money. In a world without limits, each case would be given all the time and money necessary to bring it to a successful conclusion. Unfortunately, personal injury lawyers must manage cases so that each case receives the resources to which it is entitled and so that no one case commands more resources than it deserves. That sounds easy enough, but it is not. A mistake often made by inexperienced lawyers is to misallocate resources to a case, either through over-allocation—spending too much time and money on a case—or through under-allocation—failing to give a case the resources that it deserves.

Misallocation usually results from any of the following:

1. Failing to know all the facts of the case before committing resources
2. Failing to respond adequately to new problem information discovered while the case is in progress
3. Ignoring or discounting the effect of bad facts when deciding how to allocate resources, either at the beginning or during the handling of the case

The first step in case management is determining how much time and money a case will require. The second step is deciding how much time and money the case deserves. You need to ask two questions: (1) How much will it take? and (2) Is it worth the investment? You cannot begin work on the case until you answer these questions, or you will end up spending more than you should on cases that aren't deserving and you won't be able to commit the resources to the deserving and needy cases. In most cases the lawyer advances the costs of litigation. Occasionally a client will be able to pay the costs as the case progresses. Even if the client is paying the costs, however, don't take a case if you feel that it doesn't deserve the resources.

Adopt a policy regarding advancing costs on cases. If you plan to handle "big ticket" cases like medical malpractice and products liability cases, you will have to advance costs regularly and will need a substantial credit line. Determine in advance how much you can qualify for and how much you can afford.

In even an average case, costs will add up quickly. Hospitals and medical offices charge for medical records. If your client has been treated by several doctors, has been to a hospital or two, and has seen a physical therapist, you will need to advance several hundred dollars or more for medical records. If you need copies of MRI and CT scans, that will involve a separate charge. In addition, if you need a narrative report from a physician, there will be a separate charge. If you need to meet with the physician in person, be prepared to pay between a few hundred dollars for a visit with a chiropractor or primary care doctor to a thousand dollars or more for a visit with a specialist, such as an orthopedist or neurosurgeon. Sample letters requesting medical reports and bills and a medical narrative are included in Appendix J.

Once a suit has been filed, you will have to advance costs for filing fees, process servers, depositions, and arbitration or trial fees. You may also have to pay to serve subpoenas on witnesses or records custodians at medical facilities. It is not unusual for a lawyer to advance a substantial amount of money in the course of taking even a small case to arbitration or trial in cases where doctors do not have to appear in person. If your client's doctors have to appear in person, the costs may run as high as several thousand dollars per doctor, and you probably won't be able to recover those costs from the other side even if you win. Most doctors charge slightly less if you videotape their testimony in their office before trial.

If your client is in a position to advance costs, by all means ask the client to do so. If the client can only make a small monthly payment toward the costs, ask him or her to do that. Participating financially in their case gives some people a more realistic perspective on the case than they get if you are paying all the costs.

Even if you pay all the costs of the case, send the client a periodic bill showing what you have spent on the client's behalf. If you do not send a bill, your client will have no way of knowing that you have spent anything, much less exactly how much you have spent.

Lastly, with respect to accounting for costs advanced, consult your accountant about whether you can deduct those advances as expenses on your income tax return or whether they are to be treated as a loan to the client and are not deductible.

Dealing with Bad Facts

It is easy to misjudge the effects that bad facts can have on the outcome of a case. For example, it may not seem important to you that your client has had a number of previous back injuries, but it may be important to a jury. It may not seem important to you that the defendant in your medical malpractice case is a popular small-town doctor, but it may turn the jury against your client. It may not seem important to you that the independent witness says that your client was speeding, but it could cause the jury to tag your client with 30 to 40 percent comparative negligence and reduce the verdict proportionately.

You need to identify and deal with problem facts. You must not ignore them or misjudge their seriousness. Unfortunately, many trial lawyers believe that if they tell the jurors that a certain fact is not important, the jurors will take their word for it. Don't forget that your opponents will make sure that the jury hears about the shortcomings of your case. Many trial lawyers believe that they can ignore a major problem in a case because the cumulative effect of the good points in the case will outweigh the negative ones. That, however, will depend on whether the lawyer has accurately predicted the jury's reaction not only to the bad elements of the case but to its good elements as well. Just as it is a mistake to underestimate the negative effects of bad news, it is also a mistake to overestimate the positive effects of good news.

The inexperienced lawyer will ignore the bad news or pretend that it really isn't bad news at all. The experienced lawyer will deal with it and adjust the case management plan accordingly. If all your strategies, plans, and tactics are based on a certain set of assumptions, you cannot proceed in the same way when those assumptions are proven to be wrong.

Sometimes such new information is fatal to your case. Other times, however, you can investigate and get clarification on potentially damaging information so that your case can proceed. The closer to trial that the new information emerges, the more difficult it will be for you to respond, but the worst mistake that you can make is to dismiss the evidence as being unimportant and proceed to trial.

One classic mistake is for the plaintiff's lawyer to gamble that the jury will feel such sympathy for a seriously injured plaintiff that it will overlook problems with liability. Many lawyers have turned down substantial settlement offers in cases of weak liability only to have the jury find for the defendant. By then it is too late to recognize the problems with the case. The ability to judge the potential effect of such issues accurately comes with experience, wisdom, and good planning.

Is It Worth the Investment?

Before you start spending (or perhaps borrowing) money to finance a case, you need to have some idea of what the case is worth so that you can weigh the risks against the potential rewards for your client. Your case evaluation process may be informal—asking other lawyers, friends, and family to tell you what they think about your case—but you always have to have some evaluation process. You should also consider the following case evaluation methods:

1. Case evaluation clinics sponsored by local bar groups or trial lawyer groups
2. Evaluation by a trial consultant
3. Private case evaluation performed for a fee by another lawyer
4. Focus groups

You must consider the size of the case, the budget for the case, and the complexity of the issues before deciding which method of evaluation to employ for a given case. A larger and more complex case with a larger budget will normally justify a greater expenditure for case evaluation than will the more routine, smaller case. It is important, however, that in every case you at least consider whether the case evaluation process should be informal or formal and that you note your reasons.

Since it is easy to "drift" toward trial without carefully evaluating the merits of your case, you should evaluate your cases early in the process. Even if your plan is limited to "running the case by a couple of people," you have to have all the facts available for those people to consider. Don't ask someone to evaluate a case for you, and then withhold damaging facts about your case.

Many lawyers belong to an informal network of colleagues who regularly consult with each other about their cases. These are usually solos or small firm practitioners who do not have many people in their offices to consult. You should begin to develop your own network of "consultants."

The Master Case Plan

If you have reviewed the facts and decided that you want to proceed with the case, you will need to prepare a master case plan. A sample is provided in Appendix I. Your master case plan will be the document that you and your staff, as well as your client, can refer to regularly throughout the case to determine how the case is proceeding. It will be the document against which you will compare the actual outcome of the case to assess how accurately the outcome compared with the predicted range of outcomes for the case. A master case plan will answer the question of how much it will cost to get the case to trial. It may be that after you develop a case plan, or even a preliminary case plan, you will decide against taking the case.

Summary of the Facts of the Case

The first thing to do is to summarize all facts of the case relating to both liability and damages. Helpful facts should be accompanied by potentially damaging facts. Statements of parties and witnesses should be included in the summary and should include such things as prior statements that may be introduced at trial to impeach or to contradict. If your client has given different versions of the facts of the case, it should be noted and explained as well as possible.

The elements of the claim for relief should be listed (e.g., duty, breach, proximate cause, and damages) along with a summary of the witnesses or evidence that will prove each element. If two or more witnesses have given contradictory statements or if you know that they will do so in the future, note that as well.

In a personal injury claim, the plaintiff's medical history is always a potential source of contention. In the fact summary you should include a complete summary of the client's history of medical treatment for illnesses, accidents, and injuries. If the client has made prior insurance claims or been a party to any litigation, include that information as well. In short, the fact summary should include everything that you and your staff know about every aspect of the case. If there are facts that you have not yet ascertained, be sure to note them as well and include them in your investigation plan.

Litigation Action Plan with Timetables

The effective lawyer will develop a litigation action plan for every case that is filed in court. Sometimes a lawyer will agree to take a case and will then file a lawsuit with no action plan in place. If the opposition is no better organized, the case will move toward trial in a haphazard manner. If, however, the opposition is better organized, it will take the initiative and the plaintiff's lawyer will spend his or her time reacting. A better strategy is to take the initiative whenever possible.

A litigation action plan should contain three elements:

1. Investigation plan
2. Discovery plan
3. Trial/arbitration plan

The Investigation Plan

Every case has some facts that either are disputed or are not completely agreed on. Do not assume that liability is not an issue until the other side concedes in writing that it admits liability. Moreover, just because the other side admits liability, do not assume that it is admitting that its liability was the proximate cause of your client's injuries. Many defense lawyers have had success admitting liability but denying causation. Juries can understand that concept.

You must decide at the beginning of the case exactly how you will investigate the case. Do you plan to do your own investigation? Do you have the time to do it right? If you can perform your own investigation and have the time to get it done right away, you will develop a closeness to the case that will give you a decided advantage over the other side. If, however, you put the file on the corner of your desk and don't get back to it for a couple of months, the trail will be cold. Worse yet, the other side's investigators will have gotten to the witnesses before you and taken statements that they may or may not be required to provide to you. If you have enough investigative work, you can afford to hire a staff member to perform investigations for you. Otherwise, you will have to hire an outside investigator to talk with witnesses, to take photographs of the accident scene, and to perform like tasks. Investigators normally charge on an hourly basis, but some tasks are priced on a flat-rate basis.

Sometimes, in addition to someone who can find out what was seen and heard by witnesses, the case will require more sophisticated investigation by an expert witness. Perhaps you will need to hire an accident reconstructionist to help you prove that your client was driving on the right side of the road when the accident happened or to help you prove that a tire blowout, and not your client's careless driving, caused the accident. In a medical negligence case, you must have an expert review the case to give you an opinion on whether the defendant breached the standard of care when she or he operated on your client. Magazines and other publications aimed at trial lawyers are filled with advertisements for expert witnesses arranged by category. State and local bar publications also contain such ads, and they often contain information about experts located in your area. You will need to decide in every case whether you need an expert witness to investigate certain facts and to give you an opinion on what happened from a technical point of view. Once you decide that you need an expert witness, you must then decide if the case is worth the expense.

The Discovery Plan

Plaintiffs' lawyers often view discovery as a reactive process in which they provide information requested by the other side. Interrogatories, depositions, requests for production, and requests for admission are seen as defense tools. However, the innovative plaintiff's lawyer can use those tools to gather information about the facts of the case and about the defenses that have been asserted and to limit the scope of issues in dispute.

The discovery plan should be divided into two phases: (1) responding to the other side's discovery requests and (2) preparing your own.

When you receive a discovery request from the other side, you must do the following:

1. Calendar the deadline for response.
2. Assign responsibility to a specific individual in your office.
3. Develop a plan for responding to the request.

Go over the plan with the responsible individual and decide how you will respond to each discovery item. You may need to order medical records or other documents or enlist the client's help in preparing responses to interrogatories. If you find that you cannot respond in the time allotted under your rules of civil procedure, you will either need to get a stipulation from the other side extending the response time or to apply to the court for an extension of time. The key to your discovery plan is to know how you will manage the information and how you will manage the deadlines.

The Trial/Arbitration Plan

This book does not presume to teach you how to be a great trial lawyer, but you should know that the secret of great trial lawyers is preparation and organization. It is difficult, if not impossible, to be effective in the courtroom when you are disorganized and do not know the facts of your case. If you do not know what your own witnesses are going to say, you cannot try a good case. Thorough preparation may not often turn a bad case into a good one, but poor preparation often ruins a good case.

The trial/arbitration plan for each case should contain a list of every witness you intend to call at trial and a summary of each witness's deposition testimony, the information that you plan to elicit from the witness, and the questions that you intend to ask the witness. You should note whether a witness needs to be subpoenaed for trial and whether travel arrangements need to be made for out-of-town witnesses. Your plan should also include a list of the other side's known witnesses so that you can prepare your cross-examination or arrange for rebuttal or impeachment witnesses.

In addition, your plan should include a list of every exhibit that you intend to introduce into evidence, pre-marked according to local court rules. Each exhibit should be cross-referenced to the witness through whom the exhibit will be introduced. If you anticipate any objections to a particular exhibit, you should note them and prepare your response.

Jury selection, or voir dire, should be planned in advance. The information that you would like to obtain from each prospective juror, the questions that you intend to ask, the criteria that you will use to determine whether to use peremptory challenges, and other jury issues should be analyzed in advance. If the case can justify the expense, a trial consultant can assist you in determining the profiles of those jurors you want and do not want to hear the case.

Preparation of the opening statement and closing argument should not be left until the last minute. Fortunately, your efforts to summarize the case during the case evaluation process will serve as a rehearsal of your opening statement. Of course, by the time you deliver your opening statement to the jury, you will have refined it and perfected it. The arguments that appear to be the most spontaneous and unrehearsed are often the ones that have been practiced so much that they only sound that way. The truly spontaneous and unrehearsed arguments often sound disjointed and confusing. Your trial plan must include both an opening statement and a closing argument.

Adopting the Methodical Approach

You can approach a personal injury case in one of two ways: casually or methodically. In the casual approach you won't have a plan or a timeline for getting things done. You won't have photos of the accident scene or witness statements. You will find out about key facts from the insurance adjuster rather than from your own investigation. You will find out about your client's prior injuries at deposition. Your evaluation of the case (and your settlement demand) will probably be based on incomplete information, and you will be shocked when the other side offers a fraction of what you think the case is worth. All in all, you probably will not enjoy working on the case, and your relationship with your client may suffer in the process.

On the other hand, if you adopt a methodical approach to the case and develop and follow a case plan, it will invariably go much better. Your case plan should include a timeline for each activity. Be sure to assign individuals responsibility for accomplishing specific tasks. Finally, get a good case management software program to do a lot of the hard work for you.

Essential Software for Case/Practice Management, Document Management, and Trial Presentations

10

THE GOOD NEWS FOR ASPIRING personal injury lawyers is that there is a good selection of software tools available to help manage cases; manage documents; get cases ready for settlement; and present cases at trial, arbitration, or mediation. Some products are designed for solos and small firms, while others are scalable for use by firms of various sizes. Unfortunately, there are some applications that are designed for large firms with multiple offices and are not scalable for small law offices. These are often called "enterprise" solutions. Often, the high price will tip you off to the fact that your small office is not the target market. A good rule of thumb is that if you visit a Web site for a company offering software solutions for law firms and are required to submit a request before they will give you the price, look somewhere else.

Case/practice management, litigation management, and other software packages can vary in price by hundreds of dollars for basic, low-end programs and by thousands of dollars or more for top-of-the-line programs. Personal injury lawyers who are just setting up a practice will not likely need to buy high-end applications in any category. The best advice is to try out a few programs before you buy. Most vendors offer free, fully functional time-limited demo versions that can be downloaded and worked with before purchasing. If they only offer a limited demo or only a Web-based walk, though, do not even consider their products.

Many software vendors employ an extensive network of consultants to help with installation and training. Installation and training costs can often exceed the cost of the actual program and should be factored into the overall cost of purchasing and implementing any software system. Check references and talk with other users to find out how much they spent on installation and training.

Software support charges can also add to the annual cost of any software system. Most companies offer free support for a short period, and then charge for additional support. Some charge on a per-call basis while others charge annual fees for a certain amount of support via telephone, Web, or e-mail. Find out how much support you might need and how much it will cost before purchasing.

Changing Programs

One of the factors making the choice of a case/practice management or any other system so important is the difficulty of switching from one program to another if you later decide that you are not satisfied. Even though many case management programs offer the ability to export data from their system, it is not easy to import the same data into a competitor's program without losing some data. (That may be because no vendor *really* wants to make it all that easy for you to switch to a competitor's product.) Before choosing any program, check with the vendor to find out how easy it is to export data and what programs can import *all* of that exported data. Many lawyers report that they would love to switch case management programs, for example, but do not want to have to reenter all their client and case information. Some applications make it easier than others to switch.

Case/Practice Management

Simply put, case management software provides tools to plan and track case activities from the time a new client walks in the door until the case is finally resolved.

Case Management Versus Practice Management

"Case management" and "practice management" are two different, but overlapping terms, and not everyone agrees on the definition of either. Generally speaking, a case management application (or CMS for case management system) is one that is built around a database of clients, cases (sometimes called "matters"), documents, calendar events, to-do items, and other people and organizations involved in a case. Practice management software keeps track of the same information, but also usually includes additional modules that allow integration into accounting and other functions.

For example, a case management program will normally contain a screen where you enter information about the settlement of a case, including the amount of the settlement, lawyer's fees, court costs, liens, and the like, but will not typically transfer that data directly into an accounting program where checks can be written and disbursed. A practice management program, on the other hand, will integrate case data into an accounting/check writing module so that *all* case activity can be tracked seamlessly, and it may include a module for time and billing.

Many lawyers, usually solo and small firm practitioners, prefer to keep their case management and accounting and time-and-billing systems separate. One reason is that practice management programs are often substantially more expensive than case management programs. Another reason is that many lawyers are pleased with and want to keep the stand-alone accounting/check writing program or time-and-billing program that they have been using for years and do not want to switch to something new. Many of these lawyers prefer to manage their caseload with a case management program, then use a separate software tool to write checks to pay case expenses and then disburse settlement funds from trust.

The trend in the legal software industry has been toward integrated systems. Many case management programs, even the more affordable ones, have added functionality and now offer features that were previously found only in high-end practice management applications. Many budget-priced programs now include document creation and management, time and billing, integration with e-mail programs such as Microsoft Outlook, ability to synchronize with handheld PDAs, and the ability to export to other third-party applications.

A valuable resource for keeping up to date on case management software can be found at the Web site of the Legal Technology Institute of the Levin College of Law/University of Florida (*http://www.law.ufl.edu/lti/CaseManagement/vendors.shtml*). According to Institute Director Andrew Z. Adkins III, "Law firms often underestimate what it takes to implement a computerized case management system (CMS). There is a significant investment in dollars and time required. If properly implemented, the payback and return on investment can be enormous." (*ABA Law Practice Today,* Nov. 2005)

Adkins points out that "CMS developers don't like me to say this, but most tend to agree with me: under the hood, most CMSs provide the same basic functionality." That functionality includes the following, according to Adkins:

- Rolodex or contact database
- Calendar system
- Case database
- Case notes or case diary
- Document assembly
- Reports

Case Management Programs

Some of the more popular case management programs include modules designed specifically for personal injury cases, while other programs offer a more generic interface, but are not PI-specific. Some software publishers offer different versions of their software with different levels of integration. The case management software products listed above are all "desktop" products rather than "Web-based" products that are run over the Internet via a Web server (although some may offer separate Web-based products).

Here are some of the software products (in alphabetical order) and what their Web sites say about them.

AbacusLaw® (Abacus Data Systems, Inc.) (www.abacuslaw.com): Abacus offers several versions of its software, some integrated and some not. Abacus's Web site advertises a "Classic" version for users who don't want integrated time, billing, and accounting, and "Silver" and "Gold" versions for users who want those features. Abacus advertises its ability to synchronize data with PDAs, including Blackberry.

Amicus Attorney® (Gavel and Gown Software) (www.amicusattorney .com): Amicus Attorney says that it "keeps your client matter files in familiar expansion folders where it is easy to keep things organized" and allows users to "organize all the steps on a matter, review what has taken place, plan how to proceed," and "see schedules for everything from meetings to limitation dates to deadlines and critical dates." It also allows you to "collaborate: assign tasks to colleagues, and follow up to check their status. Every event on the file is instantly put into your calendar or the calendar of those who are assigned. Review a complete chronology of every event, communication, and document."

DeNovo CaseMgr® (De Novo Systems, Inc.) (www.denovosys.com): De Novo CaseMgr says that it "makes it easy for attorneys and legal assistants to electronically manage every aspect of the case, from client intake through depositions and discovery to settlement or trial." Features include calendar/docketing, conflict management, party and case information, medical providers, insurance companies, and more. (DeNovo CaseMgr was designed by the author of this book, who has an interest in the company.)

LawBase (Synaptec Software, Inc.) (www.lawbase.com): According to LawBase, its SmartFolders™ feature provides a "unique method of automatic grouping files and matters in any manner you desire" to track cases by attorney, by subject, or any other information. Features include Case Notes, Contacts, Calendar, Interface to third party calendars and other documents, and the ability to document management suites and other applications.

Needles® Case Management Software (Chesapeake Interlink, Ltd.) (www.needleslaw.com): Needles says that it can help you to "maintain case details and motions and create customized reporting solutions." The program provides pre-set tabs for basic matter information, such as party information, case information, checklist, notes, and documents. Needles provides the capability to identify noteworthy items for quick retrieval and conflict management. Needles allows users to view and manage any letter, pleading, photograph, diagram, scanned item, or other document that needs to be viewed in the case file.

PerfectLaw® (Executive Data Systems, Inc.) (www.perfectlaw.com): PerfectLaw says that it "combines matter, contact, case, and document management in the Front Office with full-featured Back Office timekeeping, billing, and accounting to create an All-in-One® solution." The company says that it "is the only fully integrated suite that doesn't require integration with other products for timekeeper calendaring and case management." PerfectLaw Software modules for Front and Back Office include legal case management and financial management modules.

Perfect Practice® (ADC Legal Systems, Inc.) (www.perfectpractice.com/personal): Perfect Practice® says that its personal injury software "delivers client-server-based performance for large or small firm requirements. Perfect Practice includes intake-sheets, calendar/docketing with Outlook/PDA integration, contact and conflict management, status and exception reporting, imaging, e-mail integration, document merging and management, and more. It also offers lien tracking and settlement statements for personal injury firms, Integrated billing/accounting, and Notify (chat) programs."

The Plaintiff (Data Development, Ltd.) (www.theplaintiff.com): The Plaintiff advertises "a user-defined software solution that assists in the everyday practice of law and practice management." Designed for plaintiffs' lawyers, this program offers integration with Quick-Books accounting software and Palm-based PDAs.

ProLaw® *(Thomson-Elite)* *(www.prolaw.com)*: ProLaw advertises itself as "all-in-one software to automate the practice and manage the business of law. From the convenience of a Microsoft Windows desktop environment or Web browser, ProLaw automates case, relationship, and document management as well as time entry, billing and accounting—all within one integrated solution. It provides comprehensive integration with Microsoft Outlook, Word, Westlaw research, court rules, and many other popular applications to help you build and maintain a productive and profitable practice that will remain a step ahead of the competition!"

Tabs3® *and PracticeMaster®* *(Software Technology, Inc.) (www* *.practicemaster.com):* Tabs3 is a longtime time and billing and accounting package, while PracticeMaster is a newer case management and document management program from Software Technology, Inc. According to its Web site, "PracticeMaster provides an easy way for firms to create a firm-wide calendar, search for conflicts of interest, and organize case and contact information."

Time Matters® *(LexisNexis) (www.timematters.com)*: According to its Web site, Time Matters (and its companion product, Billing Matters), will manage the schedules of the entire office in real time, organize e-mail and faxes, and stop unwanted e-mail. Time Matters' features include Tasks, Alerts & Reminders; Messages, including task delegation, reminder system, and instant messaging; Contacts and Clients; Phone Calls, Cases and Matters, Mail and Courier; Documents and Forms; Notes; Billing and Expenses; Research; and an Outliner.

TrialWorks™ *(Lawex Corporation) (www.trialworks.com):* Trial-Works claims to be "considered the most technologically advanced case management software package for litigators." According to its Web site, "While TrialWorks is the only case management system designed exclusively for litigation attorneys, any type and size of law firm can benefit from its use." According to the company, "The heart of the program is the relocation of a litigator's file cabinet into your computer, using the file-folder-with-tabs metaphor that lawyers prefer. Thus, the main screen for each case has tabs for Correspondence, Pleadings, Depositions, Documents, and other relevant functions in a litigator's practice."

Other Software Tools

Document Assembly/Document Management

HotDocs® *(LexisNexis)* *(www.hotdocs.com)*: According to its Web site, HotDocs is designed to reduce the time spent generating customized documents, such as contracts, sales proposals, government and court forms, legal documents, loan applications, and medical forms. Using HotDocs, you can transform any word processor file into an interactive template by replacing the changeable text with HotDocs variables. Then, the next time you want to generate a completed document, just assemble the interactive template you've created. As you do this, you will be prompted for the information needed in the document and that information will be merged into the document. HotDocs can be integrated with databases, practice management systems, case management systems, and Microsoft® Word and Corel WordPerfect® software.

WORLDOX® *(World Software Corporation)* *(www.worldox.com)*: WORLDOX says that it "lets you describe electronic documents by filling in *profiles* as documents are created or transferred into the system. The profiles are set up within categories defined and organized based on your particular business requirements." WORLDOX also allows full-text searching, document and e-mail management capabilities, and productivity-enhancing collaboration features. The software includes a "palette of document management services," such as document check-in and check-out, version control, work lists, integrated file viewing, file activity auditing, reporting, file-level security, and more.

Litigation Support

CaseMap/TimeMap/TextMap (Lexis Nexis) *(www.casemap.com)* CaseMap makes it easy to organize, evaluate, and explore the facts, the cast of characters, and the issues in a case. CaseMap is designed for use on all types of cases and by all types of litigators and investigators. CaseMap is easy to learn and use. It features a consistent design, ease-of-use features such as live spell checking, and a prebuilt example case that makes mastering CaseMap a snap.

CaseMap links with TimeMap, a timeline-graphing tool. Users can send key facts from transcripts to CaseMap using TextMap transcript management utility. CaseMap says that it integrates with over a dozen other litigation support and electronic discovery tools including Acrobat, Binder, Concordance, iCONECT, IPRO, JFS Litigator's Notebook, KPMG's DiscoveryRadar, LiveNote, Sanction, and Summation.

Other Litigation Support Products

There are a number of other litigation support products available, but they tend to be geared toward larger firms and are far more expensive. Those products may be appropriate as your firm grows, but are likely more than a small PI practice needs. They include IBlaze from Summation Technologies (*www.iblaze.com*), Concordance and FYI 2.0 from Dataflight Software, Inc. (*www.dataflight.com*), CT Summation products from Wolters Kluwer (*www.summation.com*), and others.

Trial Presentation

Microsoft® PowerPoint (*www.microsoft.com*): PowerPoint is the presentation software component of Microsoft's Office suite of products (along with Word and Excel). Microsoft says that Power-Point allows users to "create exciting slide shows with graphics, animations, and multimedia—and make them easier to present."

Corel® Presentations (*www.corel.com*): Presentation is Corel's answer to Microsoft's PowerPoint and is a component of the Word-Perfect Office family of products. According to Corel, Presentation helps users "create stunning multimedia slide shows" and publish slide shows to PDF format. Presentation allows users to "open, edit and save Microsoft PowerPoint files."

Sanction (Verdict Systems) (*www.sanction.com*): While PowerPoint is a generic presentation program, Sanction markets itself as a "dedicated trial presentation software" and claims to be "the most user-friendly trial presentation software on the market." Sanction's Web site describes its unique features as including "Web connectivity, innovative bullet lists, and video clip editing capability."

Other Essential Software

Adobe® Acrobat® (Adobe Systems Incorporated) (www.adobe.com): Adobe's PDF format has become the standard for electronic information exchange and has been adopted by many courts as the required format for electronic filing of legal documents. Documents created in Word or WordPerfect can be saved as PDF files and then e-mailed to someone who does not use either word processing applications; the recipient can then open your document using Adobe Acrobat. Acrobat comes either as a free "reader" or as a full-featured program that allows you to open a document, "mark it up," make comments, and then send the document back to the originator or to a third party for further comment and revision.

Conclusion

Good software is an essential part of a systematized approach to managing a personal injury practice. Buying and installing software and training staff on how to use it does not have to be an expensive, complicated, and time-consuming adventure. Some software is easier to install and learn than others. Your job is to find out which programs are better than others. All the information you need is available online.

Preparing for Settlement, Arbitration, and Trial **11**

MOST CASES GET RESOLVED BY WAY OF SETTLEMENT. But by the time a case is ready for you to begin settlement discussions with the other side, you will have already invested a lot of time and will have done most of the following:

- ◆ investigated the case to understand issues of liability and comparative fault, including interviewing witnesses, police officers, and ambulance personnel, and hiring an accident reconstruction expert;
- ◆ obtained and reviewed all of your client's medical records, including records relating to treatment for other injuries;
- ◆ obtained narrative reports from treating physicians to verify claimed injuries and establish medical causation and rule out other causes of your client's present complaints;

- met with treating physicians to discuss their view of important medical/legal issues (medical causation, pre-existing conditions; other causes of complaints) and the physicians' willingness to testify in court or by video deposition;
- obtained and reviewed all of your client's employment records to determine and verify wage loss or loss of earnings claims;
- obtained and reviewed all records from other lawyers who represented your client in prior or subsequent claims or lawsuits;
- obtained and reviewed all records from insurance companies against whom your client made prior or subsequent claims;
- responded to discovery requests from the insurance company or defense counsel, including interrogatories, requests for production of documents, requests for admissions, etc.;
- researched applicable law regarding liability and damages and evidentiary issues that might arise at trial;
- reviewed all documents with your client to insure completeness;
- prepared your client for deposition by reviewing all records, explaining the deposition process and conducting a simulated deposition with your client;
- prepared your client for medical examinations by doctors hired by the defense;
- conducted a focus group or jury simulation, if warranted, to identify problem issues and establish case value;
- consulted a trial consultant, if warranted;
- explored and proposed alternative dispute resolution (ADR), including mediation and arbitration;
- discussed client's desires regarding settlement versus trial;
- prepared a settlement summary or settlement brochure as appropriate for case;
- prepared demonstrative exhibits to be used during settlement discussions, ADR, or trial; and
- determined the cost of taking the case to arbitration or trial.

This is a daunting list of activities for any law office, but for a solo or small-firm personal injury lawyer operating with minimal resources and a number of other cases, it can be overwhelming.

Plaintiffs' firms that employ a large number of associates, legal assistants, secretaries, and law clerks will have an abundance of resources to keep the case moving and to insure that the file is complete when it needs to be complete.

The general rule in PI cases is that the plaintiff's lawyer keeps things moving toward resolution. Generally speaking, the insurance company or corporate defendant and their lawyers will not take the initiative to get the case resolved. That is not always the case, of course, but the plaintiff's lawyer is always in a better position to get the other side all the information that they want or need in order to evaluate the case and make a settlement offer.

The challenge for the small firm or solo plaintiff's lawyer is that he or she will be tugged in many different directions every day. A typical day will be spent "putting out fires" and dealing with problems that must be dealt with today. That leaves precious little time to think about the case that will not go to trial until next year, but that is exactly the case that needs your attention.

If you develop a Master Case Plan and go through the planning steps outlined in Chapter 9, you may have a fighting chance to keep your head above water and avoid working nights and weekends. Without such planning, even working weekends will not bring order to your caseload.

Case management software (discussed in the previous chapter), may be what saves you and your staff and keeps your cases on track. Any good case management application will let you know what has already been done on any case, what remains to be done, who is assigned to do specific tasks, and when those tasks need to be completed. Tasks can be identified and to-do lists created, but if no one is monitoring the lists to make sure that the tasks are completed on time, your caseload will get out of control quickly.

So how, then, do you divide your time between new cases, cases that are in the middle of discovery, and cases that are ready for settlement or trial? The answer lies in having systems and procedures in place to manage the volumes of paperwork, training yourself and your staff to use the systems and follow the procedures, and paying meticulous attention to deadlines.

Any of the case management software programs described in Chapter 10 will help you get organized, but those programs will only help you if you use them faithfully.

Conclusion

IN THE INTRODUCTION YOU WERE WARNED that starting a personal injury practice probably will not make you rich. However, you were also assured that you will find plenty of opportunities to help those who are truly in need. Moreover, if you plan well and use good management techniques, you will be able to help those in need and still make a decent living. That is a goal that all lawyers should have.

If you market yourself effectively and do a good job for people, you can build a personal injury practice—even if you don't have a single client right now. You can choose to concentrate your practice on PI cases or, for variety and to even out your cash flow, you can handle other types of cases as well.

If you hire the right people and treat them properly, they will stay with you and help you build your practice. The keys to success are proper management of people and wise use of your time and money. You have to manage a law practice just as you would manage a print shop or a pizza restaurant. Most importantly, you have to treat people well.

Be prepared for the ups and downs of practice. Be prepared for the financial peaks and valleys that you are sure to encounter. Be prepared for the difficulties of dealing with people in distress. Be prepared to get fired by a client who doesn't think that you are doing enough for him or her. Be prepared to have a judge refuse your request for a continuance even though your expert witness suddenly backed out. Be prepared to be disappointed by arbitrators and juries who disagree with your theory of the case. There will be some things that you cannot control.

Once in a while, however, a jury will return a verdict that vindicates your theory of the case and gives your client the justice that she or he deserves. That will make up for all the difficult times. Once that happens, you will never again wonder if you made the right decision.

A personal injury practice is different from other types of law practice, and as stated earlier, it isn't for the fainthearted. However, if you succeed in building and managing your own practice, you won't look back on your career and wish that you had done something else. Nothing else compares. It is hoped that the suggestions contained in this book will make that building process a little easier.

Appendix A
MARKETING PLAN

GOAL 1: Attracting New Clients

Strategy 1: Online Marketing
    Tactic: Create or update Website
    Tactic: Create or update Weblog
    Tactic: Paid advertising through Web search Engine

Strategy 2: Firm Brochures & Print Media
    Tactic: Review and analyze all firm media
    Tactic: Create topical firm brochure to be distributed in office, mailed to existing or prospective client, and posted on Website
    Tactic: Hire marketing consultant

Strategy 3: Develop Relationships with Referral Sources
    Tactic: Join industry group or trade association
    Tactic: Volunteer to speak at industry group or trade association conferences
    Tactic: Write articles for industry or trade group publications

Strategy 4: Involve staff in Marketing Activities
    Tactic: Regular staff meetings on firm marketing
    Tactic: Educate staff on firm marketing
    Tactic: Develop firm wide marketing plan
    Tactic: Create incentives

GOAL 2: Expanding Into New Practice Areas

Strategy 1: Analyze profitability of existing practice areas
    Tactic: Review cases/matters, outcomes and fees
    Tactic: Study market for potential new practice areas
    Tactic: Develop plans for expanding into new practice areas

Strategy 2: Analyze market for new opportunities
    Tactic: Consult with practitioners in potential new practice areas
    Tactic: Determine barriers to entry into new practice areas
    Tactic: Create plan for entry into new practice areas

GOAL 3: Overcoming Barriers to Effective Marketing

Strategy 1: Gain understanding of obstacles to effective marketing
    Tactic:

*Include a time line for each tactic.

Appendix B

MARKET ANALYSIS: COMPETING HIGH-VOLUME PERSONAL INJURY FIRMS

Attorney/Firm	No. of Lawyers	No. of Yellow Pages Ads	Avg. TV Spots	Estimated Budget
1. _____	_____	_____	_____	_____
Comments: _____				
2. _____	_____	_____	_____	_____
Comments: _____				
3. _____	_____	_____	_____	_____
Comments: _____				
4. _____	_____	_____	_____	_____
Comments: _____				
5. _____	_____	_____	_____	_____
Comments: _____				
6. _____	_____	_____	_____	_____
Comments: _____				
7. _____	_____	_____	_____	_____
Comments: _____				
8. _____	_____	_____	_____	_____
Comments: _____				
9. _____	_____	_____	_____	_____
Comments: _____				
10. _____	_____	_____	_____	_____
Comments: _____				

Appendix C

MARKET ANALYSIS: DIFFERENTIATION FROM COMPETITORS

I. Identify the qualities or attributes that are emphasized by competitors in your personal injury market. For each quality indicate the order of importance placed on that quality by the competitor.

1. _____
2. _____
3. _____
4. _____
5. _____
6. _____

II. Identify the qualities or attributes that are identified by potential clients as being important to them. For each quality indicate the order of importance placed on that quality by the potential client.

1. _____
2. _____
3. _____
4. _____
5. _____
6. _____

III. Identify the qualities or attributes that are identified by potential clients but are not being emphasized by competitors that you could use to market your practice and differentiate your practice from the competition.

1. _____
2. _____
3. _____
4. _____
5. _____
6. _____

Appendix D

INITIAL CONTACT REPORT

Date of Contact: ____/____/____

Employee _____

Time: _____:_____

Last Name: _____   First Name: _____

Address: _____

How Did the Caller Get Referred to Us?

City/State/Zip: _____

Telephone (H): _____ (W): _____

_____ Caller Is a Present or Former Client

Caller Name (If Different):

Last Name: _____   First Name: _____

Caller's Relationship to Person Calling About:

_____ Yellow Pages
_____ Which Book?

_____

Date of Incident: ____/____/____   **Time:** ____:____

Type of Case: (Check All That Apply)

_____ Television
_____ Newspaper
_____ Radio
_____ Referral

__Automobile Accident   __Slip & Fall
__Uninsured Motorist   __Pedestrian
__Motorcycle   __Bicycle
__Defective Product   __Assault
__Claim Against Government   __Medical Malpractice

Referred by:

__On-The-Job Accident   __Minor
__Wrongful Death   __Domestic Relations
__Property Damage   __Criminal
__Traffic/DUII   __Consumer
__Contract   __Real Estate

_____
_____
_____

Office Location

_____

__Wills/Estate/Probate   __Landlord/Tenant
__Other (Specify)_____

Describe Incident: _____
_____
_____

Disposition:

_____ No Show
_____ Seen by:

Describe Injuries: _____
_____
_____

Atty: _____

Date: _____

Adverse Parties:

(1) Last Name: _____   First Name: _____

_____ Case Accepted
_____ Case Rejected

Address: _____

City/State/Zip: _____

Telephone (H): _____ (W): _____

(2) Last Name: _____   First Name: _____

Address: _____

City/State/Zip: _____

Telephone (H): _____ (W): _____

Appendix E

INITIAL CLIENT INTERVIEW

Date: _____ Referral Source: _____

Atty: _____ Legal Asst.: _____ Office: _____

BACKGROUND INFORMATION

Full Name: _____
　　　　　　　First　　　　　Middle　　　　　Last

Other names known by (including maiden name): _____
Address: _____
City, State, Zip: _____
Telephone:　Home _____ Office _____ Other _____
Date of Birth: _____ Social Security No.: _____-_____-_____
Driver's License No.: _____
Marital Status (Check One): ___Married ___Single ___Divorced
　　　　　　　　　　　　　　　　___Separated ___Widowed/Widower
Spouse's Name: _____
　　　　　　　　First　　　　　Middle　　　　　Last

OCCUPATION

Employer: _____
Address: _____
Job Title: _____ How long employed? _____
Name of Supervisor: _____ Telephone: _____
Your last date worked before illness or injury: _____
Rate of Pay: _____ Per: Month_____ Week_____ Bimonthly_____
Date returned to work: _____

INCIDENT INFORMATION

Date of Injury: _____ Time: _____ SOL: _____
Location: _____ County: _____
Weather Conditions: _____
Status: (e.g., driver, passenger, pedestrian); If passenger, who is driver? _____

Were police called? Yes___ No___ Agency: _____
Was fire department called? Yes___ No___ Agency: _____
Was ambulance called? Yes___ No___ Agency: _____
List any citations given and to whom: _____
Describe what happened: _____
_____
_____
_____
_____
_____
_____

Draw a diagram of accident scene:

INSURANCE INFORMATION

Vehicle (Year/Make/Model): _____
Plate Number: _____
Describe damage to your vehicle: _____
Location of your vehicle: _____
Property damage resolved?   Yes_____ No_____
Were photos taken? _____ Location of photos: _____
1. Vehicle in Which You Were Driver/Passenger at Time of Accident
Auto Insurance Company: _____
Address: _____
Policyholder/Insured (If Not You): _____
Policy Number: _____ Claim Number:_____
Adjuster Name: _____ Phone Number: _____
Policy Limits: _____ PIP application completed? Yes___ No___

2. Your Vehicle (If Different) or Vehicle on Which You Are Named Insured or Household Member

Auto Insurance Company: _____

Address: _____

Policyholder/Insured (If Not You): _____

Policy Number: _____ Claim Number: _____

Adjuster Name: _____ Phone Number: _____

Policy Limits: _____ PIP application completed? Yes___ No___

3. Were You On the Job at the Time of the Accident? Yes___ No___

Workers' Compensation Insurance Company: _____

Address: _____

Insured: _____ Claim Number: _____

Adjuster Name: _____ Phone Number: _____

4. Your Health Insurance Company: _____

Address: _____

Policyholder: _____ ID/Policy Number: _____

OTHER PARTY INFORMATION

Other Party #1

Name: _____

Address: _____

City, State, Zip: _____

Driver's License No.: _____

Vehicle: _____ Plate Number:_____

Insurance Company: _____ Adjuster Name: _____

Policy Number: _____ Claim Number: _____

Policy Limits: _____ Recorded statement given? Yes___ No___

Other Party #2

Name: _____

Address: _____

City, State, Zip: _____

Driver's License No.: _____

Vehicle: _____ Plate Number:_____

Insurance Company: _____ Adjuster Name: _____

Policy Number: _____ Claim Number: _____

Policy Limits: _____ Recorded statement given? Yes___ No___

*For additional defendants, use the back of this form.

WITNESS INFORMATION

Names of any witnesses: (Please include addresses and telephone numbers, if known.)

Name	Address	Phone
Name	Address	Phone
Name	Address	Phone
Name	Address	Phone

INJURIES/MEDICAL TREATMENT

List all INJURIES that you received as a result of this accident.

_____
_____
_____
_____

List the names of every **HOSPITAL** you have been seen at since the accident occurred whether *or not* you were treated for injuries caused by the accident. Include dates and reasons for each hospitalization.

Date of Admission	Hospital	Reason
Date of Admission	Hospital	Reason
Date of Admission	Hospital	Reason

List the names and addresses of all **DOCTORS** who have treated you for your injuries.

_____
_____
_____

List the names and addresses of all **PHYSICAL THERAPISTS** who have treated you for your injuries.

_____
_____
_____

Describe **every past** injury, accident, including work-related accidents, in which you have ever been involved. (Include date, time, location, type of accident, and injuries.)

_____
_____
_____

List all illnesses or injuries for which you were being treated at the time of the accident.

_____
_____

ADDITIONAL BACKGROUND INFORMATION

List every claim or lawsuit in which you have been involved in any way. Include approximate year, parties involved, reasons, and results.

_____
_____
_____

Have you ever been arrested?   Yes_____ No_____
If yes, please provide the following information:
Date: _____ Charge: _____

Have you ever been convicted of a crime?   Yes_____ No_____
If yes, please provide the following information:
Date: _____ Charge: _____
Date: _____ Charge: _____

Result (fine, penalty, etc.):_____

Have you ever filed bankruptcy?   Yes_____ No_____
If yes, please provide the following information:
Date: _____ Location:_____

Have you ever been represented by another attorney? Yes___ No___
Name: _____
Address:_____
Reason:_____

Give any other information you feel we should have to represent you effectively in this case: _____

_____
_____
_____

Appendix F

CONFIDENTIAL CLIENT QUESTIONNAIRE

Date: _____

BACKGROUND INFORMATION

1. Full Name: _____

                  First   Middle   Last

2. Other names known by (including maiden name):_____
_____

3. Current Home Address & Phone:
_____
_____

4. Employer/Business Name, Address, & Phone:
_____
_____

5. Give home addresses you have had for the past five years, including the dates of such addresses:
_____
_____
_____
_____

6. Any other additional addresses where mail can be forwarded to you:_____
_____

7. Any telephone not listed above: _____

8. Age:_____ Weight:_____ Height:_____
   Date of Birth:_____ Place of Birth:_____
   Social Security Number: _____
   Drivers' License Number:_____
   Marital Status: (Check One) ___Married ___Single ___Divorced
                        ___Separated ___Widowed/Widower

9. Spouse's Name: _____
　　　　　　　　First　　　　Middle　　　　Last

10. Children:

Name	Address/Phone	DOB
Name	Address/Phone	DOB
Name	Address/Phone	DOB
Name	Address/Phone	DOB

OCCUPATION

11. Name of your current employer, address, how long employed, and name of supervisor.

_____

_____

12. Names and addresses of previous employers for past five years. (Please state dates of employment, type of work, and reasons for leaving.)

_____

_____

_____

13. Name and address of spouse's current employer and how long employed.

_____

_____

14. Your last date worked before illness or injury: _____
　　　Rate of pay: _____ per: _____
　　　Date returned to work: _____

15. If your job changed after illness or injury, indicate new job or duties and reason for change. _____

_____

_____

_____

16. Do you have available for the past five years your income tax records showing your earnings for those years? _____ If yes, please provide copies to our office.

INCIDENT INFORMATION

17. Date of injury: _____ Time: _____
Weather Conditions: _____

18. Location: _____ County: _____

19. Describe what happened.

_____

_____

_____

_____

_____

20. List the name and address of other party.

_____

_____

_____

21. List any witnesses, other than yourself, whom you feel might be helpful to your case. Please include addresses and telephone numbers, if known.

_____

_____

_____

22. Did you authorize or send medical reports to anyone relating to this accident? If so, please give names, addresses, and date authorization was sent.

_____

_____

23. Did you make any statements to anyone concerning this accident? If so, please state to whom, date, circumstances, and if you made or signed any written statements.

_____

_____

_____

24. List all illnesses or injuries that you received as a result of this accident. _____

_____

_____

_____

25. List the names and addresses of all doctors who have treated you for those illnesses or injuries described in question 24.

_____

_____

_____

26. When is your next doctor's appointment?

        Dr. Name: _____ Date: _____

        Location: _____

27. Describe every past injury accident, including work-related accidents, in which you have ever been involved. (Include date, time, type of accident, and injuries.)

_____

_____

_____

_____

_____

28. List the names and addresses of all doctors you saw in the past ten years before the accident. (Please include the reason you saw them and what treatment they prescribed, if any.)

_____

_____

_____

_____

29. List all illnesses or injuries for which you were being treated at the time the accident occurred.

_____

_____

_____

_____

HOSPITALIZATION

30. List the name of every hospital you were in during the ten-year period before the accident occurred. (list the dates and reasons for each hospitalization.)

_____

_____

_____

_____

31. List the name of every hospital you were in since the accident occurred (whether or not you were treated for injuries caused by the accident). Include dates and reasons for each hospitalization.

_____

_____

_____

_____

32. List every surgical operation performed since the accident occurred.

_____

_____

_____

_____

PROBLEMS RELATED TO ACCIDENT

33. List every illness or injury which you believe was caused or made worse by the accident.

_____

_____

_____

_____

34. List and describe all other expenses due in any way to the accident.

$ _____

$ _____

$ _____

$ _____

ADDITIONAL PERSONAL BACKGROUND INFORMATION

35. List every injury or illness not already mentioned that you have ever had for which you saw a doctor, and the approximate year in which each occurred.

_____

_____

_____

36. List every claim or lawsuit in which you have been involved in any way. (Include approximate year, parties involved, reasons, and results.)

_____

_____

_____

37. If you have ever been arrested for any reason, list
Date: _____ Charge: _____
Result (fine, penalty, etc.): _____

38. Have you ever filed for bankruptcy? _____
If so, give dates: _____

39. Give any other information you feel we should have to help us represent you in this case.

_____

_____

_____

_____

40. Give the names and addresses of two people who will always know where to reach you.

_____

_____

_____

Date completed: _____, 19__.

I certify the above information to be true and complete to the best of my knowledge and belief.

_____
(signature)

Appendix G

CLIENT SERVICE QUESTIONNAIRE

How were you referred to (Firm Name)?
TV commercial _____ Yellow Pages _____
Referred by a friend ___ Know lawyer or staff personally _____
Other (please explain)_____

Why did you select (Firm Name)?
___ Convenient location
___ No recovery/no fee
___ Home & Hospital visits
___ Firm handled an earlier case for me
___ Other (please explain)
_____
_____

What is your opinion about the following?

	Very Satisfied	Somewhat Satisfied	Somewhat Dissatisfied	Very Dissatisfied
1. Convenience of the office location				
2. Getting through to attorney on the phone				
3. Attorney returned phone calls				
4. Attorney explained things clearly				
5. Courteousness				
6. Staff helpfulness				
7. Keeping me informed				
8. Amount of settlement				
9. Attorney fee				
10. Attorney met with me when I wanted				
11. Attorney seemed concerned about me as a person				
12. Attorney believed in my case				
Overall, what is your level of satisfaction with (Firm Name)?	**Very Satisfied**	**Somewhat Satisfied**	**Somewhat Dissatisfied**	**Very Dissatisfied**

Do you feel you could have handled your case as well without an attorney? Yes____ No____

Would you ask (Firm Name) to handle another case for you? Yes____ No____
If no, please explain: _____
_____

Would you refer a friend to (Firm Name)? Yes____ No____
If no, please explain: _____
_____

THANK YOU FOR TAKING THE TIME TO COMPLETE OUR CLIENT SERVICE QUESTIONNAIRE. PLEASE FEEL FREE TO CALL OUR OFFICE AT ANY TIME IF WE CAN BE OF SERVICE TO YOU.

Appendix H

TASK ASSIGNMENT

CATEGORY	TASKS	RESPONSIBLE PERSON	TIME REQUIRED
1. Human Resources Management	Hiring, training, evaluating, scheduling, etc.		
2. Financial Management	Budgeting, accounting, tax planning, payroll.		
3. Office Operations	Space planning, purchasing.		
4. Technology Management	Computer & technology planning and acquisition, on-line services, library.		
5. Strategic Planning	Development, implementation, and monitoring of short-term and long-term plans for the practice.		
6. Marketing & Client Development	Development and implementation of marketing plan, the production of media, planning and giving of speeches or CLE presentations, advertising.		
7. Case Management	Client intake, referral, case processing, client relations, deposition and discovery, litigation management.		
8. Trials & Alternative Dispute Resolution	Preparing for, trying, and mediating cases.		

Appendix I

MASTER CASE PLAN

INITIALS DATE   TASK

Initial Telephone Contact

_____ _____ Initial phone screening
_____ _____ Enter caller into database
_____ _____ Check for conflicts
_____ _____ Letter (case not accepted)

Initial Conference with Lawyer/Legal Assistant

_____ _____ Initial conference
_____ _____ Letter (case not accepted)
_____ _____ Fill out new client/new matter intake form
_____ _____ Contingent fee agreement signed
_____ _____ Medical authorization forms signed
_____ _____ Employment authorization forms signed
_____ _____ Confidential client questionnaire reviewed

File Opening

_____ _____ Create new hard-copy file
_____ _____ Enter new client/matter into database
_____ _____ Enter statute of limitations into database and calendar
_____ _____ Enter other deadlines into database and calendar

New Matter Work-Up

_____ _____ Send initial letters to adverse parties/insurance companies
_____ _____ Application for benefits form completed
_____ _____ Contact potential lien holders
_____ _____ Order medical records and billings
_____ _____ Order prior medical records and billings
_____ _____ Order records from prior claims
_____ _____ Prepare investigation plan
_____ _____ —Obtain witness statements
_____ _____ —Accident investigation/reconstruction
_____ _____ —Visit accident scene if necessary

154

_____ _____ —Photos of vehicles/other photos
_____ _____ —Contact expert witness
_____ _____ Wage loss verification

30-60-90 Day Follow-Up
_____ _____ Personal contact with client re: medical status
_____ _____ Follow up prior requests
_____ _____ Status letter to adverse parties/insurance companies/lien holders

When Client Is Medically Stationary
_____ _____ Order closing narrative reports
_____ _____ Order final medical records and billings
_____ _____ Meeting with client
_____ _____ Verify medical bills lien amounts

Settlement
_____ _____ Review and summarize medical information
_____ _____ Review and summarize accident information
_____ _____ Review and summarize applicable law
_____ _____ Prepare settlement proposal
_____ _____ Get client approval of settlement proposal
_____ _____ Conduct settlement negotiations
_____ _____ Coordinate disbursements after settlement

Litigation
_____ _____ Prepare litigation plan
_____ _____ Draft pleadings
_____ _____ Coordinate filing of complaint and service of summons
_____ _____ File and respond to motions
_____ _____ Prepare discovery plan

Depositions
_____ _____ Identify deponents
_____ _____ Schedule depositions
_____ _____ Take and defend depositions
_____ _____ Order transcripts
_____ _____ Summarize depositions

Other Discovery

_____ _____ Prepare discovery requests

_____ _____ Respond to discovery requests

Trial/Arbitration

_____ _____ Set case for trial (if necessary in jurisdiction)

_____ _____ Schedule pretrial conference with judge (if necessary)

_____ _____ Schedule witnesses for trial/arbitration

_____ _____ Prepare subpoenas

_____ _____ Subpoena medical records for trial

_____ _____ Subpoena employment records for trial

_____ _____ Prepare client for trial

_____ _____ Contact trial/jury consultant (if necessary)

_____ _____ Prepare trial order

_____ _____ Prepare pretrial motions (if necessary)

_____ _____ Prepare trial memorandum

_____ _____ Prepare jury instructions

File Closing

_____ _____ Update information in database

_____ _____ Close file

_____ _____ **Other Activities:** _____

_____ _____ _____

Appendix J
SAMPLE LETTERS FOR A PERSONAL INJURY PRACTICE

Referral Thank-You Letter

Name
Address

Dear _____:

Thank you for referring _____ to me/our office. I met with him/her/them this week.

Many times people are hesitant to refer their friends and family to lawyers because they think that we are too busy to take new clients. We welcome referrals and encourage people to make referrals to us. I can truly say that the best clients I have served over the years have been those who were referred by my friends and colleagues and by satisfied clients.

I appreciate your confidence, and we will give special treatment to anyone referred by you.

Sincerely,

Initial Letter to Client

Name
Address

Dear _____:

Enclosed is a copy of your signed Fee Agreement, along with copies of the initial correspondence that we have sent out in your case. I would advise you not to talk to anyone about your accident except us and your own insurance company. If anyone else wishes to talk to you, have them call our office.

You should send any medical bills and prescription receipts that you receive to your own auto insurance carrier once a claim is established. They will pay as many of your bills as possible under your personal injury protection coverage as well as reimburse you for your prescriptions. Please send us copies of any bills you receive before sending them to your insurance company for payment.

It is also important to keep a record of any other expenses you may have in connection with your accident. You should keep us informed as to how your medical treatment is progressing and let us know right away when your doctor releases you from his or her care.

If your doctor takes you off work at any time, always obtain a disability slip from him or her. This will help if you will be making a wage loss claim with your insurance company. Please provide our office with copies of any disability slips you may receive.

Please do not hesitate to contact our office with any questions or concerns about your claim. The legal assistant working with me on your claim is _____. He/She is well informed about your case and will be able to assist you promptly.

Be sure to keep us posted of any change in your address or telephone number.

Thank you for retaining our firm to represent you.

Sincerely,

Letter Turning Down Case

Name
Address

Re:

Dear _____:

This will confirm that, although we discussed your recent accident claim, this office will not be representing you in connection with the above referenced matter. If you wish to pursue this matter, you should contact another lawyer right away. In the meantime, I will be doing nothing further on your behalf.

If you do not have another lawyer in mind to represent you, I would suggest calling the State Bar Lawyer Referral Service at _____. That agency maintains a list of attorneys who are available to discuss your type of case.

You should be aware that the statute of limitations in a personal injury claim runs _____ years from the date of the accident, or [statute date]. This means that if you have not settled your claim or filed a lawsuit by [statute date], you will be forever barred from doing so.

Thank you for contacting our office.

Sincerely,

Letter to Client re: Rejecting
Settlement and Filing Lawsuit

Name
Address

Dear _____:

This will confirm that you have instructed me to reject the insurance company's offer to settle your injury claim for $_____ including medical bills of $_____. Since the insurance adjuster has indicated that this is their top offer, and you do not wish to accept the offer, we will proceed to file a lawsuit.

Before we file, we want you to be aware of the costs involved in a lawsuit. The filing fee in District Court will be $_____. We will then have the lawsuit papers (the Complaint) served on the defendant(s) and the fee for service of the complaint will be a minimum of $_____ per defendant. Once the case is filed, the attorney for the other side will probably want to take your deposition and I will want to take the defendant's deposition. The fees for the depositions could be anywhere from $_____ to _____.

If the case goes to trial, we will be required to call one or more of your doctors to testify, either in court or on videotape. The cost of each doctor's appearance will be approximately $_____. It is my estimate that total court costs will be approximately $_____. If we win, you will be entitled to recover some, but not all, of those costs from the other side. If we lose, you will be obligated to pay a portion of the other side's court costs.

It will take approximately ____ months for your case to get to trial.

Please call me if you have any questions.

Sincerely,

Letter to Witness to an Accident

Name
Address

Dear _____:

This office has been retained to represent _____, who sustained personal injuries in the above-referenced auto accident. I understand that you were a witness to this accident.

I would appreciate it if you would take a moment to call me and discuss with me what you saw. If you need to call me in the evening or on a weekend, my home telephone number is _____.

I look forward to hearing from you.

Sincerely,

Request for Medical Bills

Name
Address

Re: Our Client/Your Patient:
     DOB:
     Date of Accident:
     Patient/Chart No.:

Dear Sir or Madam:

Our firm represents the above named individual in a claim for personal injuries as noted above. Enclosed with this letter is a signed Authorization and Consent for Release of Information, which permits you to release information to our office in connection with this case.

I would appreciate your sending me a copy of any and all billings for services rendered to our client in connection with these injuries.

Thank you.

Sincerely,

Request for Narrative Report

Name
Address

Re: Our Client/Your Patient:
       Date of Accident:

Dear Dr. _____:

This office represents _____ in connection with a claim for injuries resulting from an automobile accident that occurred on _____. We have previously provided you with a medical authorization that permits you to release information to us in connection with this case.

[Client name] informs me that you now consider [him/her] medically stationary. At this time, I would ask that you submit a narrative summary outlining the injuries received, treatment rendered, and your prognosis with regard to our client's injuries. If you anticipate any permanency or chronic recurrence of symptoms, I would appreciate your so advising me.

Please also provide an itemized statement of your services for [client name]. If you require prepayment for these services, please advise our office by telephone, and we will immediately forward our check.

Thank you for your cooperation and assistance in this matter.

                              Sincerely,

Letter to Medical Provider Agreeing to
Pay Medical Bills Upon Settlement

Name
Address

Re: Our Client/Your Patient:
DOB:
Date of Accident:
Patient/Chart No:

Dear _____:

Our firm represents _____ in a claim for personal injuries arising out of an accident on the above referenced date. The attorney handling this claim is _____. We are currently pursuing a claim for damages on behalf of our client _____. [Insert * or **.]

*We are in the process of completing our investigation and hope to avoid the necessity of a lawsuit.
OR
**A lawsuit was filed on [date of filing].

At this time, we cannot precisely predict when this case may be completed. However, we are making every reasonable effort to resolve this matter as soon as possible.

We have been authorized by our client to protect your charges in the amount of $_____. It is further agreed that this account will be satisfied out of any amounts received, whether by way of settlement or judgment. Please note that this does not constitute an agreement by this firm or the individual lawyers in this firm to be legally responsible for payment of any medical bills.

Please indicate in writing whether these terms are acceptable to you. If you have any questions, please contact the undersigned.

Thank you.

Sincerely,

Request for Medical Records

Name
Address

Re: Our Client/Your Patient:
DOB:
Date of Injury:

Dear Dr. _____:

This office represents the above-referenced client in a claim for personal injuries sustained on the above noted injury date. Please provide copies of the following:

_____1. Chart notes/records (include patient history, lab reports, medication records, etc.) relating to the injuries received by our client

_____2. Itemized bill/ledger

_____3. X-rays

_____4. Other:

Please contact our office if you have any questions or need any additional information. A signed authorization is enclosed which allows you to release information to our office.

Thank you for your assistance.

Sincerely,

Representation Letter to Insurance Company re: Uninsured Motorist Claim

Name
Address

Re: Our Client/Your Insured:
      Date of Loss:
      Claim No.:

Dear Sir or Madam:

Our firm has been retained to represent your insured, [client name], in a claim for personal injuries arising out of an injury accident with an uninsured motorist occurring on the above-mentioned date.

Please note our representation in this matter and direct any future inquiries or correspondence regarding this claim to this office. Additionally, if our client has previously executed any release forms, please be advised that the authority granted by those documents is hereby rescinded.

Please also provide us with transcripts of any statements that our client may have given to your company with regard to this accident.

Please contact the undersigned at your earliest convenience to discuss the liability and damages in this case.

We look forward to your courtesies and assistance in this case.

Sincerely,

Representation Letter to
Adverse Insurance Company

Name
Address

Re: Our Client:
       Your Insured:
       Date of Loss:
       Claim No:

Dear Sir or Madam:

Our firm has been retained to represent the above-named individual in a claim for personal injuries arising out of an injury accident with your insured on the above mentioned date.

Please note our representation in this matter and direct any correspondence regarding this claim to this office. Additionally, if our client has previously executed any release forms, we hereby rescind the authority granted by those documents.

Please acknowledge receipt of this correspondence at your earliest opportunity.

Thank you.

                                   Sincerely,

Index

The Lawyer's Guide to Marketing Your Practice, Second Edition

Edited by James A. Durham and Deborah McMurray
This book is packed with practical ideas, innovative strategies, useful checklists, and sample marketing and action plans to help you implement a successful, multi-faceted, and profit-enhancing marketing plan for your firm. Organized into four sections, this illuminating resource covers: Developing Your Approach; Enhancing Your Image; Implementing Marketing Strategies and Maintaining Your Program. Appendix materials include an instructive primer on market research to inform you on research methodologies that support the marketing of legal services. The accompanying CD-ROM contains a wealth of checklists, plans, and other sample reports, questionnaires, and templates—all designed to make implementing your marketing strategy as easy as possible!

The Lawyer's Guide to Marketing on the Internet, Second Edition

By Gregory Siskind, Deborah McMurray, and Richard P. Klau
The Internet is a critical component of every law firm marketing strategy—no matter where you are, how large your firm is, or the areas in which you practice. Used effectively, a younger, smaller firm can present an image just as sophisticated and impressive as a larger and more established firm. You can reach potential new clients, in remote areas, at any time, for minimal cost. Learn the latest and most effective ways to create and implement a successful Internet marketing strategy for your firm, including what elements you need to consider and the options that are available to you now.

The Lawyer's Guide to Increasing Revenue: Unlocking the Profit Potential in Your Firm

By Arthur G. Greene
Are you ready to look beyond cost-cutting, and toward new revenue opportunities? Learn how you can achieve growth using the resources you already have at your firm. Discover the factors that affect your law firm's revenue production, how to evaluate them, and how to take specific action steps designed to increase your returns. You'll learn how to best improve performance and profitability in each of the key areas of your law firm, such as billable hours and rates; client relations and intake; collections and accounts receivable; technology; marketing and others. Included with the book is a CD-ROM featuring sample policies, worksheets, plans, and documents designed to aid implementation of the ideas presented in the book. Let this resource guide you toward a profitable and sustainable future!

The Lawyer's Guide to Creating a Business Plan: A Step-by-Step Software Package

By Linda Pinson
A well-written business plan can provide the road map to greater profitability for any law firm. But where to start? *The Lawyer's Guide to Creating Your Business Plan* is a complete, easy-to-use Windows®-based software package that will help any lawyer research and write a winning business plan for a new or existing firm. Based on Linda Pinson's award-winning *Automating Your Business Plan,* this software package has been designed specifically for lawyers so you can make the right decisions for a successful and profitable business future. It's a step-by-step stand-alone program that takes you through your entire financial plan while the program sets up and formulates all your financial spreadsheets, and does all your calculations for you. The end result is a professional business plan that will be readily acceptable by potential investors, partners, etc. The program is supplied on a CD-ROM with a short instruction manual. A bonus PDF of the acclaimed book *Anatomy of a Business Plan,* is also included on the CD-ROM.

Through the Client's Eyes: New Approaches to Get Clients to Hire You Again and Again, Second Edition

By Henry W. Ewalt
This edition covers every aspect of the lawyer-client relationship, giving sound advice and fresh ideas on how to develop and maintain excellent client relationships. Author and seasoned practitioner Henry Ewalt shares tips on building relationships and trust, uncovering some unlikely ways to make connections in addition to traditional methods. Marketing techniques, including brochures, newsletters, client dinners, and sporting events are discussed. Other topics that are covered include client intake, client meetings, follow-up, dissemination of news, fee setting and collection, and other client issues. Completely revised and updated, including information on using e-mail communications and more.

How to Start and Build a Law Practice, Platinum Fifth Edition

By Jay G Foonberg
This classic ABA bestseller—now completely updated—is the primary resource for starting your own firm. This acclaimed book covers all aspects of getting started, including finding clients, determining the right location, setting fees, buying office equipment, maintaining an ethical and responsible practice, maximizing available resources, upholding your standards, and marketing your practice, just to name a few. In addition, you'll find a business plan template, forms, checklists, sample letters, and much more. A must for any lawyer just starting out—or growing a solo practice.

Collecting Your Fee:
Getting Paid From Intake to Invoice
By Edward Poll

This practical and user-friendly guide provides you with proven strategies and sound advice that will make the process of collecting your fees simpler, easier, and more effective! This handy resource provides you with the framework around which to structure your collection efforts. You'll learn how you can streamline your billing and collection process by hiring the appropriate staff, establishing strong client relationships from the start, and issuing client-friendly invoices. In addition, you'll benefit from the strategies to use when the client fails to pay the bill on time and what you need to do to get paid when all else fails. Also included is a CD-ROM with sample forms, letters, agreements, and more for you to customize to your own practice needs.

How to Draft Bills Clients Rush to Pay,
Second Edition
By J. Harris Morgan and Jay G Foonberg

The authors take you step by step through the process of building the client relationship, setting the appropriate fee agreement, and drafting the bill that will get you paid. You'll find, in plain language, a rational and workable approach to creating fee agreements and bills that satisfy your clients, build their trust, and motivate them to pay. Comparisons and samples of fee agreements and invoices are integrated throughout the text, along with a clear explanation of which methods work best—and why.

The Successful Lawyer: Strategies for Transforming Your Practice
By Gerald A. Riskin

Available as a Book, Audio CD, or Combination Package!

Global management consultant and trusted advisor to many of the worlds' largest law firms, Gerry Riskin authors this comprehensive and inspirational book conveying practical and helpful solutions to make your practice not only more profitable, but far more satisfying. Whether you're a novice or seasoned lawyer, no matter the practice setting, *The Successful Lawyer* provides you with valuable road-tested advice that is immediately helpful and rewarding. Discover how to transform your practice into a more exciting, fulfilling, and profitable one. Dare to dream! If you're looking for ways to enhance your current practice, allowing you both added income and increased satisfaction, then look no further.

Law Office Procedures Manual for Solos and Small Firms, Third Edition
By Demetrios Dimitriou

This revised and updated edition provides you with everything you need to develop and compile a succinct, comprehensive procedures manual, geared toward the unique management issues of a solo or small firm. This step-by-step guide offers direction on setting policy and procedures for your firm, and provides sample language and documents, both in the text and on the accompanying CD-ROM, to allow for easy customization. Proper implementation of sound policies and procedures will help ensure your firm operates effectively, efficiently, and productively, resulting in not only a professional environment for your firm, but optimal delivery of legal services to your clients.

Flying Solo: A Survival Guide for Solo and Small Firm Lawyers, Fourth Edition
Edited by K. William Gibson

Revised and completely updated, the fourth edition of this comprehensive guide includes practical information gathered from a wide range of contributors, including successful solo practitioners, law firm consultants, state and local bar practice management advisors, and law school professors. This classic ABA book first walks you through a step-by-step analysis of the decision to start a solo practice, including choosing a practice focus. It then provides tools to help you with financial issues including banking and billing; operations issues such as staffing and office location and design decisions; technology for the small law office; and marketing and client relations. And, the final section on quality-of-life issues puts it all into perspective. Whether you're thinking of going solo, new to the solo life, or a seasoned practitioner, *Flying Solo* provides time-tested answers to real-life questions.

Marketing Success Stories: Conversations with Leading Lawyers, Second Edition
By Hollis Hatfield Weishar and Joyce K. Smiley

This practice-building resource is an insightful collection of anecdotes on successful and creative marketing techniques used by lawyers and marketing professionals in a variety of practice settings. Whether you work in a firm of 1 or 1,000, these stories of marketing strategies that paid off will inspire you to greater heights. You'll gain an inside look at how successful lawyers market themselves, their practice specialties, and their firms. Learn from your colleagues what really works, and how to incorporate these winning initiatives into your own practice!

30-Day Risk-Free Order Form
Call Today! 1-800-285-2221
Monday–Friday, 7:30 AM – 5:30 PM, Central Time

Qty	Title	LPM Price	Regular Price	Total
_____	The Lawyer's Guide to Marketing Your Practice, Second Edition (5110500)	$79.95	$89.95	$_____
_____	The Lawyer's Guide to Marketing on the Internet, Second Edition (5110484)	69.95	79.95	$_____
_____	The Lawyer's Guide to Increasing Revenue (5110521)	59.95	79.95	$_____
_____	The Lawyer's Guide to Creating a Business Plan (5110528)	149.95	179.95	$_____
_____	How to Start and Build a Law Practice, Fifth Edition (5110508)	57.95	69.95	$_____
_____	How to Draft Bills Clients Rush to Pay, Second Edition (5110495)	57.95	67.95	$_____
_____	Collecting Your Fee (5110490)	69.95	79.95	$_____
_____	The Successful Lawyer—Book Only (5110531)	64.95	84.95	$_____
_____	The Successful Lawyer—6 Audio CDs, Boxed Set (5110537)	129.95	149.95	$_____
_____	The Successful Lawyer—Audio CD and Book Combination Package (5110533)	174.95	209.95	$_____
_____	Law Office Procedures Manual for Solos and Small Firms, 3rd Edition (5110522)	69.95	79.95	$_____
_____	Flying Solo, Fourth Edition (5110527)	79.95	99.95	$_____
_____	Marketing Success Stories, Second Edition (5110511)	64.95	74.95	$_____

*Postage and Handling	
$10.00 to $24.99	$5.95
$25.00 to $49.99	$9.95
$50.00 to $99.99	$12.95
$100.00 to $349.99	$17.95
$350 to $499.99	$24.95

**Tax
DC residents add 5.75%
IL residents add 8.75%
MD residents add 5%

*Postage and Handling $_____
**Tax $_____
TOTAL $_____

PAYMENT
❑ Check enclosed (to the ABA)
❑ Visa   ❑ MasterCard   ❑ American Express

_____
Account Number   Exp. Date   Signature

Name _____ Firm _____
Address _____
City _____ State _____ Zip _____
Phone Number _____ E-Mail Address _____

Guarantee
If—for any reason—you are not satisfied with your purchase, you may return it within 30 days of receipt for a complete refund of the price of the book(s). No questions asked!

Mail: ABA Publication Orders, P.O. Box 10892, Chicago, Illinois 60610-0892
♦ **Phone: 1-800-285-2221** ♦ **FAX: 312-988-5568**

E-Mail: abasvcctr@abanet.org ♦ **Internet: http://www.ababooks.org**